LET IT GO

MANIFEST WHAT YOU REALLY WANT BY GIVING UP AND ALLOWING

DREW ROZELL, PH.D.

very cool life

CONTENTS

Preface   vii

PART I
Introduction   3

PART II

LET IT GO
It's All Good   31
What You Decide From Here Is All That Matters   35
Be Willing NOT To Have It   39
It's Going To Get Better From Here   44
Stop Resisting Your Own Thoughts   47
Stop Resisting Your Thoughts About Other People   51
Be Willing   53
A King Commands   57
Dare To Fail   61
Keep It Simple   66
Be Vulnerable   69
Embrace The S Word   73
The Right Thing Ain't Always   77
Take A Nap   80
Control, No. Direct, Yes   84
Let The Universe Sort Out The Details   90
No Need To Prove Yourself   94
Decide   98
Your Purpose In Life: Have Fun!   102

Acknowledgments   107
Did You Like This Book?   109
Yes, I Will Personally Coach You   110

For my children, Alex and Ella, who remind me to let it go every day.

PREFACE

My promise is to help you let go so you can allow your desires — whatever those desires may be — into your life. Them's big words. Ones you've likely heard before, and likely to less than satisfying results. Whether you allow yourself to have it all is up to you. But I am not overstating the case when I tell you that I chose to write this book because I believe that **letting go can serve as the simplest, easiest, most efficient way for you to get out of your own way and begin allowing your deepest desires to finally show up in your life.**

This book is a guide for manifesting and deliberately creating your life according to your specific desires and preferences. Getting what you really want is not only possible when you raise your awareness and start making some new decisions, it's normal.

I've made my living as a professional life coach for over two decades. It's the only real job I've ever had. My job is to offer people a radical sense of clarity about how they can make their lives feel freer, easier, and more connected. To impart these ideas to those who want them (and certainly to improve my own life), I've spent hundreds of hours studying metaphysical principles, chiefly The Law of Attraction. During this study, I've come across many ideas, concepts, methodologies, and practical exercises. However, as wonderful as I find all this information, none of it is very useful unless it's applied. I find that when there's too many options of things I could do, it's more difficult to focus and apply any one idea. And, without application, well, nothing much happens no matter how good the intentions.

I've always resonated with Leonardo Da Vinci's observation that simplicity is the ultimate sophistication. I'm drawn to efficiency; I want to find the simplest, easiest, and fastest way to get the job done. In the study of Attraction, I see many people who become enamored with all the ideas, but fail to find a point of focus and apply it. The result is that nothing much changes and they end up wondering whether any of this attraction stuff really works. Seeing this pattern, I immersed myself with the intention of pulling out a single thread that can be applied in many different contexts, one that holds all of these wonderful ideas together. I want to share the power of applying **one clear (and fun) idea** that serves as the catalyst in your creating and allowing your deepest desires to come into your experience.

Soon after getting clear in my own desire, I found myself in Burlington, Vermont, leading one of my Very Cool Life live events and coaching a member of the audience. As I talked, the words I'd been looking for came out of my mouth.

The key to having what you really want is simply dropping resistance.

There it was, the one idea that could be applied over and over, in so many different contexts. I scribbled a note to myself to make sure I didn't lose the idea. Over the next year, I began paying attention to the most enjoyable manifestations taking place around me (my own and those of my friends and clients), seeing how all of these creations were the direct result of letting something go.

PART I

INTRODUCTION

Yes is the answer and you know that for sure

Yes is surrender, you got to let it go

— John Lennon, from the song Mind Games

THE KEY to having what you want — anything that you want — is your willingness to let that thing go.

This may sound like familiar advice as you've probably heard some spiritual teaching advocating the power of non-attachment. However, though these words sound good, you likely notice that the advice is rarely put into practice. This is not surprising when you stop and think about it. Consider that other than possibly presenting the concept, no one taught you much of anything specific regarding the awesome power of letting go. No one ever told you what it means to let go or what letting go really feels like. No one ever explained the metaphysics of why letting go makes practical sense for you to get what you want. And as attractive as letting go might sound, it's likely no one offered any real-world examples and applications of how to let go in your life.

This book is designed to change that. My job is to take this ethereal, *sounds-good-but-how?* concept of letting go, giving up, and relaxing your way to your desires and to make it a simple, grounded, strategy that you can apply to every area of your life.

Let's begin with a few examples on the subjects of money, relationships, and well-being. I'll start with a story about money and my career.

EXAMPLE #1: MONEY

Years ago, I found myself in bed, unable to fall asleep, deeply worried about not having enough money. In my mind, I had good reason to fret. After years of having a full coaching practice, my entire client base suddenly dried up. Clients left and there was no one new in the pipeline. My income was about to plummet. I had just closed on a house. While I loved my new home, I'd never taken on such a hefty financial obligation. The process of becoming a homeowner stirred my dormant fears about all the awful things that would happen if I ran out of money. Now, I was about to find out.

My mind was consumed with dark thoughts — everything I'd created to date was a sham. I'd never get another client. I'd have to get a real job. I'd lose my house to the bank. And the worst part of all of this? As a public figure in the world of personal development, it felt as though the whole world would be witness to my failure.

Every day, I'd try to fight off my negative thoughts. I'd try my best to stay positive. I'd write down affirmations: *I am abundant in every way.* And of course, right out of the playbook of the desperate, I scrambled around, following the facile advice of the motivational crowd to take massive action. In this case, I repeatedly mailed my list, offering them great deals on my services in hopes that they would rescue me from my impending financial cliff.

But the affirmations did nothing. Despite slashing my fees, no new clients came. And no matter how hard I tried to dam off my negative thoughts, worry drowned me.

Nothing was working. I was out of ideas. Torturing myself with worry felt miserable. Then, I reached my breaking point. I couldn't take living in a state of constant worry for another minute, so I made a decision. I decided that nothing was worth feeling this bad, not a house, not my reputation, and certainly not money. I shoved my chair away from my desk. "Fuck this!"

Fuck it. Fuck it all.

Take the house. Take all my stuff. Take my career. Take my reputation.

While I'd danced around these thoughts before, this was the first time I allowed myself to think them. I walked around my house and I began to imagine selling off my possessions for money. I imagined selling my cars, my furniture, and my canoe. I imagined calling my real estate agent and asking her to sell my house. I allowed myself to think these awful thoughts that I'd been terrified to entertain previously. In allowing myself to hit the cellar of my fearful thoughts, and to finally look these thoughts straight in the eye, I immediately felt a wave of relief.

Things were going to be okay.

Once I gave up in my struggle with money, and connected to the thought that I'd be okay, lighter thoughts flowed in...

I've lived without money before... And I still managed to have a pretty damn good time...

Somehow I always land on my feet...

Sure maybe I'll lose some money, but when I sell the house, I'll get a lot of my equity back into my bank account. I'll have several years of living expenses covered.

Even if my coaching gig is over, I know how to run a business now. I can easily start a small lawn care business that would pay my bills.

Things always work out for me in the end.

Within a couple weeks of allowing myself to imagine losing everything and being accepting of this scenario, (not liking it, but rather being okay with it), the money started to flow again. And that intense fear around money has never returned. When I do experience the occasional pang of worry about money, I say Fuck it! right away without having to relive the drama of torturing myself. Remembering to let go in this way never fails to provide both an immediate feeling of relief, as well as re-opening the gates and allowing money to flow to me.

Through this experience, I discovered that the key to having the money I wanted in my life was my willingness to let it go.

EXAMPLE #2: RELATIONSHIPS AND BABIES

A friend and his wife were having trouble conceiving a child. Approaching 40, with every month they became more worried and desperate. After trying every other thing they could think of, they turned to the medical world. And yes, looking from the outside in, they approached this pregnancy issue as a problem that needed to be fixed. Tens of thousands more dollars later and two rounds of the latest fertilization techniques, there was still no baby. The doctors told them they could try again, but they were told the odds of Sara getting pregnant were negligible.

Heartbroken, out of money, and too emotionally drained to face another disappointment, they gave up. While it didn't feel good for them to quit, it felt better than continuing. Jason told me that after the second attempt failed, they decided, "Hey, we gave it our best shot. So maybe we will never have children, but we can still have a great life together. And who knows? Maybe somewhere down the road we'll adopt or something. But right now we're giving up. We've had enough of this."

Within the next year and a half of letting go of their plans and no longer trying to fix what they considered broken, his wife delivered a healthy baby girl (conceived and delivered naturally). Overjoyed, Jason and Sara considered this to be a miracle and a fluke. But, while every pregnancy is a miracle, they began to believe this was no fluke. In fact, they really started to believe in the power of letting go when Sara (at 42) delivered their second healthy girl two years later.

EXAMPLE # 3 BODY AND HEALTH

My friend Jon gained a lot of weight after college. As a result he had trouble sleeping, back problems, and high blood pressure. He confided in me, sharing his discomfort and how he wished he could rid himself of the extra pounds he'd been dragging around. However, in the next breath, he'd tell me how he believed his weight issue to be genetic. He wanted to change his situation, but remained unwilling to believe that there was anything he could to do to facilitate such a change.

One night I hosted a party where Jon met another of my friends, Howard. Howard was a therapist counseling people before they underwent weight reduction surgery. When Jon discovered this, he asked Howard if he would be a candidate for surgery. Howard calculated some body mass numbers, and indeed, at his present weight, Jon would qualify for the surgery.

While it may sound odd, this thought brought Jon a feeling of relief. He could see a potential solution to his problem where he could not find one before. Inwardly, he allowed himself to say, "Oh, well... I can just give up the fight and get the surgery someday," and ease his self-loathing. By connecting to a thought that brought him relief, and just allowing himself to just be a fat guy, something very cool happened.

In less than two years, Jon shed over 60 pounds. Like most people when they saw him transforming, I asked the question, How'd you do it? Jon's reply was a completely unsatisfying, "Oh, I dunno. It's really not that hard."

When pressed he'd elaborate, saying how he made some changes, sure, but each change felt like the next natural thing to do. He said he began exercising because now it felt better to move his body when it previously felt like a chore. He gradually started eating higher quality foods and then discovered that he preferred eating crisp vegetables more than cheeseburgers delivered though a window. With each pound he lost, he gained more momentum. As we were finishing up the discussion, Jon reflected, "You know, I suppose everything started changing after I had that conversation with Howard."

It's important to note that Jon didn't struggle, fight, or will his way to a new body. That's why he had trouble explaining his own process. Also, the fact that his weight came off easily contradicted the most popular narrative in our culture: We're conditioned to believe that we need to suffer before we're worthy of our desires. While heroic stories of overcoming over-whelming odds make for sexier, more dramatic tales than saying, "Oh, I just decided to give up and let go!" not only is letting go the easier path, it's also much more effective.

In this specific example, Jon has remained trim for five years, with no signs of ever going back. Compare this with the success rate of dieters and others who fight against their weight and witness the glaring flaw of the motivational/willpower approach.

Again the key to having what you want — anything that you want — is your willingness to let that thing go. In this example, by just allowing himself to imagine taking the easy route of surgery, Jon became willing to end the war against his fat.

Letting go is everything you think it is. It's giving up. It's allowing and surrender. It's releasing yourself from heavy thoughts like worry.

You'll feel the power of letting go when you divorce yourself from the old ideas about who you're supposed to be. You'll feel the power of letting go when you give up fighting against unwanted circumstances. You'll feel it when you take the leap into vulnerability, and drop your hidden defenses. You'll feel the power of letting go when you decide to feel the full range of your emotions.

The power of letting go comes from consciously dropping your resistance to feeling good in this moment, and deciding to have what you want, *right now*, just because you want it.

To leverage an idea, it's important to take the concept from a theoretical idea to a something concrete. While you likely understand what I'm talking about in terms of letting go of resistance and moving into the place of allowing, it's not really very powerful and practical until you can *feel* it.

WHAT IT FEELS LIKE TO LET IT GO

Relief.

That's it. When you find yourself stuck on some unpleasant

thoughts or facing some unwanted situation, the right thought is the one that allows you to *feel just a little bit better.*

Certainly there are many variations in the feeling of relief, but they all feel lighter than the thought right before you decided to let go. To be clear, if you're coming to this focused on something that feels very heavy to you, it's unlikely that letting go will transport you to a state of lightness. The gap between those two feelings is just too wide. However, when you pay attention, you'll notice that the surrender thought will allow you to feel lighter (if only a little bit), than you did before. Frustration is better than despair.

When you choose to let go instead trying to fix a problem or turn your attention away from something you don't like, this will usually allow you to connect to a better thought. Now this is important because all of your thoughts have *momentum.* By connecting to a thought that brings you relief, you begin the process of climbing out of the hole you stumbled into. Better feeling thoughts attract better feeling thoughts. This is how the Law of Attraction works. It works without fail. It's **your job to leverage this power by directing your thoughts in the wanted direction**.

WHAT LETTING GO DOES NOT FEEL LIKE

Now that you're clear that letting go always feels like relief, it's worth mentioning what it does *not* feel like. We need to distinguish it from those times when you're thinking something like, "Fuck them! I don't care what they think!" In these instances, as Shakespeare might say, "Thou doth protest too much." Despite what you say, you really do care what someone else thinks and you're using strong words as a shield to protect you from someone else's opinion. But when you start paying close attention in your life, you'll also notice that whenever you raise a defensive shield to protect yourself from something you really don't like, the perceived attacks and the unwanted experience will continue. Instead of letting go, you're really resisting, focused on fighting off the thoughts that you DON'T like about someone.

As long as you're trying to protect yourself from something or someone in this way, you will not be allowing yourself to change your reality in the way you want it to be. Conversely, change comes with the feeling of vulnerability and defenselessness.

In this case the thought would be something like, "Well, I really don't like what this person thinks about me. But I have no control over what any one else thinks. I can let them think whatever they want to think about me and move on with my life."

Leveraging the power requires awareness, willingness, and practice, but when you choose to drop your resistance, you allow yourself to feel better. The better you allow yourself to feel, the more you become a cooperative component in allowing the wonderful things you want.

Also, it's important to note that the letting go feeling is clearly distinct from reacting to something you don't like and saying, "*Whatevvver, dude...*" like a surly teenager. When you're pretending not to care about something that you really do care about, you're still hooked.

Pretending not to care is a very subtle way of protecting yourself against the potential future disappointment of not getting something that you truly want. In this case, a more constructive thought would be something like, "I really want this thing. And even though I really want it, in this moment I am willing <u>not</u> to have it." You see, when you're truly willing NOT to have something you want, you immediately feel the relief of letting that thing go. Paradoxically, being willing to let it go means you drop your resistance and bring your desire closer to you.

In both the previous examples, the feeling of resistance is present, either overtly or subtly, and resistance always feels tight. So remember, when you're invoking the power of surrender, you will always feel the presence of *relief*.

RELIEF IS ALWAYS ONE BREATH AWAY

I highly encourage you to bring this theoretical concept down to personal level. One simple way to instantly connect is through your breath. Inhale as deeply as you can, hold that breath for a moment, and exhale fully. And just like that, doing something you've done millions of times throughout your life, you connect to the visceral feeling of letting go.

For me, letting go feels like taking my worries and whatever I've been wrestling with, inhaling all of them, blowing them out and into the sky and deciding that whatever I want is handled. Lots of times when I make this decision, I hear John Lennon's *I'm Stepping Out*...

Woke up this morning, blues around my head

No need to ask the reason why

Went to the kitchen, and lit a cigarette

Blew my worries to the sky

Here's the next verse of the song. I share them because they perfectly capture the vibration of letting go and I am a big fan of using songs to activate specific feelings.

If it don't feel right, you don't have to do it

Just leave a message on the phone and tell them to screw it

After all is said and done, you can't go pleasin' everyone

So screw it...

Some of the variations of relief you might feel when aligning include:

- Relaxation
- Surrender
- Ease
- Clarity
- Freedom
- Peace
- Connection

It might also be helpful to think back to a time when you mustered the courage to give up on something (maybe a relationship, a career path, a goal, an idea about who you are supposed to be, etc.) and connect to the memory. Allow yourself to take a few moments to bask in the feeling you experienced when you let go of something that looked right on the surface, but you knew didn't feel right.

Got that feeling? (Nice, right?)

Well, keep this memory in your back pocket so you can easily recall it and reconnect with this lighter feeling when you find yourself pushing up against life in ways that do not feel good to you.

In fact, you might just want to practice this feeling over and over for the simple reasons that 1) it feels great to do so, and 2) when you're not resisting, you are allowing, and everything you want comes to you when get out of your own way and you allow.

HOW THE POWER OF LETTING IT GO WORKS (LET'S GET METAPHYSICAL!)

To understand and the leverage the power requires you to begin to consciously apply one of the most basic principles of physics into your life.

Resistance slows everything down.

Because the force of resistance slows everything down, when you eliminate resistance in your life, the faster and easier you allow yourself to experience the manifestation of your desires. So while this basic understanding of how eliminating resistance is the key to having what you want, it's worthwhile to briefly recap the nature of how things get created in your experience.

EVERYTHING YOU WANT IS FLOWING TO YOU, ALWAYS

The manifestation of your desires — each and every one of them, big or small, with no exceptions — is the natural order of things. When you ask for something out of desire, that thing is always granted to you because the Universe operates like a predictable, mechanical fulfillment machine.

The Universe doesn't have opinions or feelings about your desires and it does not judge your worthiness or hold back for any reason. Whatever you focus upon gets created for you instantly and is then sent out for delivery to you. However, for this delivery to reach you, your job is to be a vibrational match for what it is that you've asked for. If you simply expect your desire to show up, it does. If you think about your desire in a resistant way (i.e, you *hope* it shows up, you *worry* about it showing up, you try to control *how* it shows up), its manifestation becomes much less likely.

In thinking about the mechanics of this, imagine a sparkling stream flowing through the woods. Picture yourself standing on big rock in the middle of this stream, watching the water pass by. Now imagine this: As soon as you have a desire swell up within you, whether that desire be for a sandwich, an extra $150K, or a new lover, that desire is created for you.

The moment you imagine something, the manifestation of that desire splashes down in the water, not far upstream from where you're standing, but just around a bend. While you can't see it yet, you can be sure that the stream is doing its job, effortlessly carrying your desire down to you. Your only job is to relax and stay in the knowing and clear expectation that what you want is on the way. In a very short time, your desire will float right to you and all you have to do it pluck it from the water. Remember, this whole manifestation business is simple and you are already a master. You do this all the time.

Look up from this book and notice everything that surrounds you in this moment. YOU created all of it. At some point, before you experienced the physical version of your desires, *you imagined it.*

For example, when I look around me, I see the Green Mountains of Vermont. Now before deciding to have this house in my experience, I spent some time imagining what it would be like to have a mountain view. Likewise, when I see something "smaller," like the glass of lemon water on my desk, it's clear that the water is there because a short time ago I briefly imagined how good it would be to have some cold water with lemon. Imagination precedes manifestation and yes, you do this all the time.

WHEN YOU EXPECT IT, IT'S YOURS

It's important to note that when your expectations align with a desire, you manifest that desire more quickly. Back to my lemon-water example, I felt thirsty, went to my kitchen, grabbed a lemon, a glass, and some ice and then turned the knob on the kitchen faucet. Voilà! Water appeared and I had my drink.

Certainly you've done the same and you very likely don't even think of this as a manifestation of a desire; you're so tuned to the magic of hot and cold water appearing on demand (right in your home!) that you don't think of this as a big deal. Running water has been part of your experience for so long that you have a very powerful, clear expectation that when you go to the sink and turn on the faucet, water flows out.

Now consider this fact… Around the world, there are billions (billions!) of people who do not share your clear expectation for an endless supply of clean water delivered on command. They are not in the habit of imagining such a thing. As long as something is unimaginable, it cannot be manifested. But because you've likely always had the experience of water on demand, you can imagine it. You have no resistance to the idea that when you turn a knob, water will come out, even though you likely have no idea how the water reaches you. You manifest in this same effortless way with the vast majority of your life's desires.

The reason you tend not to think of yourself as a master manifestor is that it's certainly easier to focus on those desires that have not yet come into your experience. Very often, we consider these desires to be "bigger," things you've wanted for a long time, but never seem to show up. And the longer you go without realizing your desires, the more frustrated you tend to feel and the less you likely practice imagining having what you want. Let's go back to our stream to better understand what's taking place when our desires seem to elude us.

YEAH, BUT WHERE'S MY STUFF?

Think of something you'd really like to experience right now. It could be anything... A pile of money in your bank account, a good night's sleep, a healthy body... anything. Got it?

Now notice that as you picture your desire, there's currently some thoughts that run contrary to your having what you want right in this moment. There's some reason you believe you cannot or should not have it right now, otherwise it would be in your experience. This is not a big deal, and you can certainly change it (that's the whole point of this book), but it's good to have this foundational understanding of the metaphysics at work in the creation of your desires.

With every thought that runs contrary to your desire, picture yourself throwing a boulder in the middle of the water, just upstream from the rock you're standing on. The more boulders you throw in the middle of the stream, the more likely the things flowing on the water are going to get stuck before they reach you. What you want has been created, it's trying to reach you, but it's held up on the obstacle you've created. (The exception would be when your desire is just so powerful the water flows over the boulder.)

Now it's worth noting that you will experience all of your desires. This will happen when you free yourself from all resistance, and guess what? This is what death really is — the obliteration of all resistance. So when you decide to check out of this physical experience, you get to experience the essence of all your desires. Hooray!

But do you really want to have to wait until you die to experience what you really want? Of course not. And the really good news is that you don't have to. In fact, you don't have to wait a minute longer to have what you really want.

The only thing that's ever in your way of manifesting any desire you have are those boulders you're tossing upstream — the thoughts and beliefs you're focused on that run contrary to your desires. There is no *thing* or no *one* stopping you except some old habits of thought.

With a little focus and some letting go, the world is indeed yours. When you drop your resistance to having what you want, it flows to you. When you get out of your own way and simply allow what you want to come into your life, your desires manifest. There are no exceptions to this Law of the Universe.

THE KEY IS DROPPING YOUR RESISTANCE

So now that you know that the only thing in between you and anything you want is your resistance to having it, the next question you're likely asking is rather obvious...

What's the fastest, easiest way to drop my resistance?

Well, I'm glad you asked! Because all the groundwork has led us to this inevitable conclusion...

The fastest, easiest way to drop your resistance is to come down with a big 'ole case of the fuck-its and start allowing yourself to let go in relation to your desires. It's really about coming back into alignment with the tremendously powerful creator you really are. And you're ready for that, aren't you?

Even if something is totally not clear to you (or you really want to believe all of this, but just don't quite yet), that's fine. Read on and allow yourself to take any information that resonates with you. Leave the rest.

In just a moment, we'll start exploring some specific, practical ways that you can begin to leverage the power of letting go in just about any area of your life. Before we get into that level of depth, I want to frame those essays by addressing a couple important points.

First, if this approach is as fantastic and effective as I claim it to be, then why isn't everybody practicing it?

Second, in order to get the maximum benefit of the words that follow and begin to directly apply them to your life, there's a few pre-requisites you'll need to abide.

Here are a couple questions for you...

1) Growing up, was the foundation of your education built off the belief that *your life was meant to be easy?*

I bet your answer is no. Life's a bitch, and then you die.

2) Were you ever taught that the real key to getting what you want is letting go?

I'd wager the exact opposite to be more likely. If you wanted to be successful you needed to persevere at any cost.

People don't practice the power of letting go because it's contrary to everything they've been taught about getting what they want.

We're taught to value being busy. We're taught that in order to have something we want, we need to suffer for it first by doing things we'd really rather not do. *That's just life in the real world.* And then we start to believe this to be true. (Footnote: In the past I'd have clients who came to me telling me how unhappy they were, that they had no fun, no magic. In the next breath they'd tell me how they worked 80 hours a week, often with a hint of pride. Even though they were miserable, they could wear their incessant busyness and suffering like a badge of honor.)

We're taught to value persistence and commitment. We're taught that giving up is a form of weakness. We're taught to stifle our feelings and intuition in favor of logic. We're taught to play it safe and live like everyone else. We don't live our lives in the unique way that feels best to us. As my friend Frank Butterfield says, we're taught to eat our mushy peas before we can have any ice cream.

Now's here's the thing about how the Law of Attraction works... Whatever you believe, **you are always right**. Law of Attraction will always show you more of exactly what you believe to be true. (So you'll want to be *very* conscious of what you assert to be true.)

If you've taken on the belief that you must make some sacrifice in order to have what you want, then that is what your life will show you again and again. Likewise if you believe that you came into this life to "learn lessons" you will create many rather unwanted experiences that allow you this. Your creations will always match your beliefs and you'll certainly have the evidence and the stories to back up your assertions.

But the cool thing about beliefs is that you are free to change them at any moment. And when you deliberately start to assert *what you really want to experience*, once again, you are always right. Law of Attraction will bring you the people, circumstances, and opportunities that perfectly match your new belief.

When you take in the fact that you are always right, doesn't it make a whole lot more sense to start declaring that your life is easy? And fun? And that your desires flow to you, just because you want them to?

Of course, it does.

But old habits can be stubborn. Old patterns of thought become well-worth paths and in the unfolding of life events, it's often easier to just keep doing what we've been doing than to make a new, conscious decision. It's easier to think that life is supposed to be an uphill battle, as most people believe, than to embrace the radical idea that life is supposed to be easy.

So yes, in the context of our culture, the idea that letting go, giving up, and relaxing could be the key to creating your desires will likely remain a radical idea for some time. But when you begin implementing this power in your life, to quote a client of mine, you'll have so many delightful moments of your life unfolding in just the perfect way that you'll have the pleasure of saying "this shit works!"

THE PREREQUISITES FOR MAKING THE POWER OF LETTING GO WORK FOR YOU

Letting go is the key for allowing your desires to come into your experience. This is a simple theoretical concept, but not always easy to apply.

In order to see the kinds of manifestations you've wanted for a long time, there are a few pre-requisites that you'll have to meet. Some of these you may have handled long ago, others might feel like a leap. In either case, you're going to want to pay attention to these ideas and draw them close to receive maximum benefit.

PRACTICING RADICAL RESPONSIBILITY

For you to experience the power of letting go, you'll want to adopt the perspective that through your own free will, you are the creator of all of your experiences.

All of them. 100%. No exceptions. Zero. Zippo. Zilch.

You're even the creator of all the things in your life that *you really don't like*. In my book *The Very Cool Life Code*, I call this practicing Radical Responsibility for your life. If you believe that bad things just happen to you, it's likely you will dwell in feelings of resistance and resentment. As long as you're pushing against things you don't like, you will perpetuate more of these unwanted experiences.

REMEMBER THAT HOW YOU FEEL DETERMINES WHAT YOU CREATE

In order to really leverage the let-it-go mindset, recognize the fact that we live in a vibrational universe — everything is energy. You get what you feel. Let me remind you why remembering the vibrational nature of the universe is so important.

In order to see the manifestation of your desires, you must be a match on the feeling-level for what you are asking for. You figure $100,000 in your bank account would relax you, but unless you feel relaxed FIRST, the money will not (and cannot) come to you. And it's hard to find a lover if you don't feel adored now, before the person shows up.

It's really just math. How You Feel = What You Create.

Things have to add up. Here are some other general examples:

You cannot suffer your way to ease.

You cannot stress your way to happiness.

You cannot worry yourself to your desires.

You cannot work your way to relaxation.

You cannot earn your way to freedom.

You cannot sacrifice yourself to abundance.

So, if you're noticing that you're not creating what you really want, change how you are choosing to feel.

If you can embrace (and continually remember) the fact that how you feel determines what you get, you're on your way to being able to leverage really leverage the power of letting go.

YOU MUST BE WILLING TO CARE ABOUT HOW YOU FEEL ABOVE ALL ELSE

In order to feel the relief of letting go there are a couple prerequisites. First, you **must be willing to raise your awareness of how you feel in any given moment**. Second, and just as important, as you raise your awareness of how you feel, **you must choose to care about how you feel**. You must be willing to choose to consciously and selfishly (in the best way) allow yourself to follow what feels better to you in any given moment. While you might read this and say, "Well of course, I care about how I feel!" I'd bet that upon closer inspection, you've been conditioned to let your feelings and preferences to take a backseat to numerous influences of your culture (e.g., being polite, being nice, being liked, being in "integrity," putting the desires of other people ahead of your own, and so on).

My job here is to raise your awareness to where and why you are ignoring your intuition. In turn, your work is to apply this awareness and **allow yourself to make your decisions based on what feels better to you**. As you might expect, reorienting yourself around your feelings, preferences, and desires will take some practice, but you're ready for that. Right?

THIS IS A PRACTICE (NOT A QUICK FIX)

While this approach to your life is simple to understand, I'm not offering you a quick fix. In fact, nothing needs fixing at all.

Here's why…

If you possess the perspective that you have some problem in your life that needs fixing (e.g., you don't have enough money, you're not as successful as you should be, etc.) your focus is on the problem rather than your desire. That math will never add up.

Approach these ideas as a practice. Allow yourself to marinate in the concepts for a while. See which ideas feel better to you, and then experiment with applying them when you feel inspired to do so. Say *I give up* when it feels better to do so.

Remember, this book (or any book) won't really change your life. Books and ideas alone do not really have that power. What changes your life is *the implementation of ideas*, and sure, these ideas are very often found in books. What you choose to do with this book is totally up to you, but if your desire is to make your life feel even better (rather than just being entertained), see these ideas as a way of amplifying the greatness of your cool life.

A disclaimer: **you will never be done with feelings of resistance in this lifetime**. Resistance is part of the human experience and it's not to be avoided or eliminated (in fact, trying to protect yourself from resistance will only create more of it).

Resistance serves an essential purpose in that it is always there to clarify the most direct path to your new desires. By providing the contrast that shows you what you DON'T want, resistance allows you to clearly define what want right now (which is surprisingly hard for people to define).

So resistance is there to be leveraged. Think of those rumble strips on the side of the highway. When you drive over those, the vibration is uncomfortable and provides clear feedback that you are veering off course. The bumpy ride reminds you to adjust course. Leveraging resistance requires you to sensitize yourself to the feelings as they arise, and then to move in the new direction of your desires. Out of habit (and a lack of responsibility), most people dwell in resistance, forgetting that they always have the power to adjust course and allow themselves to start having what they want now.

The work here is in deliberately living your life in the raised state of awareness during which you notice all the places you're still choosing to swim against the current for no other reason other than this is what you did the day before (and the day before that).

Letting go requires you to be awake, to look inward, to notice what feels easier, and to allow yourself to walk in that direction. It's a practice, not a solution.

So don't be fooled, living consciously is work. In fact, it's THE work.

LIVING THE ABNORMAL LIFE

In the beginning of *The Very Cool Life Code*, I make the point that a Very Cool Life is an *abnormal life* and the same is true here. When you decide to let go and move into your own alignment, while you will be very much going with your own flow, you can't expect other people to be floating down the river with you.

Most people are not at the point where they're interested in letting things be easy. They're more accustomed to *seeing their lives as happening to them*, rather than exploring how wonderful it is experience yourself as a *deliberate creator*. None of this is wrong in any way. Whatever someone desires, it's exactly right for him or her. That said, as you progress into your own alignment you will make new decisions.

When you start to let it go and relax your way into your desires, it's okay if other people, even those very close to you, do not understand. (Don't be surprised if later on they're asking you how everything started to come to you so easily.)

You'll also notice that the decisions you begin to make will feel abnormal to you as well. To be clear, in no way should they feel bad, but rather they will feel different, expansive, and new. It's like using a new operating system on your computer. At first it takes a little getting used to, but you will adapt very quickly, in large part because your new decisions will feel better.

When you live with the power of letting go, you will be running counter to a culture that's bombarding you to work harder, to strive for the next rung, to never, ever give up. This will all go really well for you if other people think you are weird and it makes you smile.

Letting go is the Swiss army knife of personal evolution tools. When you start applying this universal power, you'll see how this radical approach produces what you want in your life.

Now, the lecture ends and the entertainment begins. Enjoy.

PART II

LET IT GO

IT'S ALL GOOD

"*NOTHING IS FUCKED, Dude... Nothing is fucked... Come on, you're being very undude.*"

-- Walter, John Goodman's character in *The Big Lebowski*, consoling The Dude, played by Jeff Bridges.

I CAN'T TELL you how many times this line is repeated around my household. It's one of our favorite mantras.

Nothing is fucked here... Nothing is fucked, dude.

Just thinking about those words and typing them here makes me feel good. And while it might sound silly, when my kids are using the wall as a coloring book, remembering that nothing is fucked loosens me up immediately. And do you know why this is the case?

Because it's TRUE!

Nothing is fucked. Ever. No matter what's going on around you.

No matter what's on the news. No matter what's (not) in your bank account. No matter what anyone else wants you to believe.

If you could always see your life from the full perspective of who you really are — your higher self — you'd never forget this. But you didn't come into this physical experience to have a perfect life. That'd be really boring. You came here to grow, to experience, and to have your desires evolve. And all that requires you to bump into and off of stuff from time to time. It's no big deal and just how the mechanics of your life are set up.

The greater truth is that All Is Well. Always. You will create things in your life that you don't like, of course. Again, that's natural. But in the end, **you can't do life wrong.** Let me say that again because I see so many people trained to be perfectionists in their approach to life get so hung up on this point...

No matter what you're doing, you can't get life wrong. Ever. Nothing is fucked. Ever.

Right now you're having a physical experience, but you're not a physical being. You're a vibrational being, an energetic being who is having a physical experience. And one day, when you're done here, you'll go back to your non-physical state of total well-being.

When you die, there will be no Supreme Being with a snowy white beard and a pair of Birkenstocks judging your worthiness with a clipboard. There are no tests to pass. You are whole, complete, and perfect right now. Your inner light is a thousand times brighter than the brightest star in the universe. Hell, you are literally made of stardust. You are the Universe.

So while you're here, decide to have some fun, okay? That's the whole point... And to do that, you're going to need to lighten up and remember that all is well.

While the concept that all is well is simple to understand (and certainly feels good to contemplate), it is **The Leap**. This is where you have to make a conscious choice about your life and the world around you, often with dog shit on your shoe.

Here's the thing about the metaphysical laws of our universe… Where you focus your attention over time becomes your belief. What you believe becomes your reality. While this is likely not a new idea for you, the real point here is to remember that you manifest whatever you believe to be true, and so you are always right.

If you choose to believe that the world is fucked, guess what, you're right! As you move through life you would see the evidence all around you that perfectly reflects and supports your belief.

Conversely, if you believe that is all is well, and that things always work out for you, hey, you're right too! Working tirelessly on your behalf, the universe orchestrates very cool outcomes on your behalf.

Of course, these are just words and words do not teach. Only direct experience teaches. If you want to leverage the infinite creative powers of the universe, the powers that wait to do your bidding like the best concierge that ever existed, you'll need to be willing to make The Leap. Leave the masses and make All Is Well your default belief.

Most often, making this Leap means distancing yourself from your current reality. Now remember that in your current reality, the "good" and the "bad" all reflect the thoughts you've been choosing to think in the recent past. Without a doubt there are things in your life right now that you don't like very much. It's very easy to point at the things that you don't like and think,

"This kinda sucks…" or "This is WRONG! I hate this! Get away from me!"

While this is a common strategy, metaphysically speaking, this approach is doomed. The problem isn't that you've created something you don't like (as we'll see in later sections, all your desires spring directly from the contrasting experiences of what you don't like), the problem **is that you're choosing to resist your unwanted creation**. And yes, when you resist something, the thing you don't like will persist until you stop resisting.

The antidote is simple: Remind yourself that nothing is fucked and that all is well. Connect yourself to the feeling of relief associated with those thoughts. Take a few moments to connect to some better-feeling thoughts (whatever they may be) that will allow you to let go of your resistance and reconnect with your true magnificence. Directing your thoughts in this way is the real work. Choosing to make The Leap to seeing your life as perfect (even when it's not) is the real work. Removing yourself from the "ain't it awful!" conversations with family and friends is the real work.

So as you go through your day, you'd be well served to assert that All Is Well. When you hit some turbulence, remind yourself that *nothing is fucked here, dude.* Know you cannot get it wrong. Nothing and no one is out to get you. In fact, everything and every one is here to help you, when you allow it.

When you can move through your life with this orientation, knowing that it's all good, you've set the foundation that will allow you to let more and more resistance go and begin to allow more of what you really want.

WHAT YOU DECIDE FROM HERE IS
ALL THAT MATTERS

ONE OF THE most important aspects of leveraging the power of letting go is also one its more challenging aspects.

Specifically, I am asking you to look at your creations, particularly the ones you don't like very much, and offer a big *"oh well"* to the fact that they exist. I'm challenging you to look at something you see in your current reality, something perfectly real, and say, *This really doesn't matter much.*

Because what you see before you is really a reflection of your past. And the past is over. Finis. Done.

How you created something or why you created it might be interesting, but it's not at all relevant to your future. **The only thing that's relevant in any given moment is your decision of where you wish to direct your life from the present moment.**

So, what do you want from this moment forward?

I'll get back to the importance of deciding in a minute, but first let's talk about what draws our focus away from our desires.

The tendency for most people is to look at their unwanted creations and then begin to analyze them.

Why did this happen? *How* did this happen? *Where* did I go wrong? And this makes perfect sense. We've been trained that the best way to avoid making the same mistake in the future is to turn around, retrace our steps, and find the spot where we went off course.

However, by doing this you are condemning yourself for creating something unwanted and operating from a place of resistance. When you are looking back to something that you consider a failure and you try to make sense of how things unfolded, whether you're aware of it or not, you are likely doing so with the intention of wanting to avoid a similar outcome in the future.

But resistance is resistance. And because we live in a Universe where only vibration matters (and not good intentions), what you resist persists.

Examining things you don't like only increases the likelihood that you will create more of the same-feeling unwanted creations. This is Metaphysics 101. While "those who fail to learn from the past are condemned to repeat it," sounds logical enough, from a metaphysical perspective it's total bullshit. Quite simply, the rule of the universe is that whatever you focus on expands. So if you're combing through recent events, trying to pinpoint where you went wrong, while you may come up with an answer that satisfies your logical mind, you're choosing to perpetuate the energy of the problem.

Remember everything you see before your eyes in this moment is a perfect reflection of where your focus *was* a short time ago. Your present experiences reflect your *past* thoughts. So going back to dwell is never helpful. To leverage the power of letting go, you'll want to stop resisting your unwanted creations and start deciding what you want from here.

Years ago on a snowy day I decided to take my dogs for a walk in some nearby woods. I loaded them into my truck and shortly thereafter T-boned a car after I slid across the road on an elbow turn. While no one was hurt (I'd been driving only a few miles an hour), I did significant damage to both vehicles. After the shock of the collision wore off, I began chastising myself for being so stupid to venture out when the roads were slippery.

I'd created this accident. And I didn't like it for all sorts of reasons, chiefly among them that it was going to cost me money and I'd messed up my beautiful truck.

My initial reaction was to look back and chastise myself for my decisions.

I never should have gone out in the snow...

If I'd only gone another way...

How could I have been so stupid?

Damning thoughts towards ourselves and our creations are super common. In fact, they tend to be our default response in the face of unwanted outcomes. We're our own harshest critics, dusting the competition. If you're looking for examples in your own life, look to where you are choosing to dwell in the feelings of guilt, regret, self-loathing, unworthiness, or frustration.

After a while I got tired of beating up on myself. I just said what's done is done. And then I remembered to ask myself the key question...

What do I want from here?

My truck was a classic model Toyota Land Cruiser. You don't see many on the road. It was a special vehicle for me. I'd bought it on the West Coast, and after a few Northeast winters, some rust spots started to pop up. I'd been wanting to get it back into showroom condition for the past year, and now that I'd be putting some money into fixing my vehicle, I decided to use this as an opportunity to restore the truck to its original condition.

As soon as I got home from the accident, I hopped online and started searching for parts for my truck. I found a great resource that had beautiful aftermarket products for my vehicle. Along with a new hood and door, I ended up finding a new style kit with some flashy bumpers and matching mirrors. With a few more clicks, I discovered a local auto wizard who would put everything together for me and become a trusted resource for years to come.

So while I got into an accident, I decided to make the event the catalyst to allowing myself to have something I was really wanting — my vehicle to look great and for me to feel great driving it again. When you create something unwanted, take the opportunity to get clear on what you're wanting in the present moment.

You will always create things you don't like for as long as you live. **Creating things you don't like is what provides you with the contrast and the clarity to choose what it is that you are wanting from here.** I cannot overstate the importance of this point. Because if you're resolute on condemning yourself for creating unwanted outcomes, you will likely never make the leap to use the contrast for its intended purpose — deciding what you will have from here.

So then next time you create something you don't like (and no, it won't be long), the remedy is to ask yourself the only question that matters...

What do I want from here?

BE WILLING NOT TO HAVE IT

I LOST MY SUNGLASSES YESTERDAY.

They cost about $200. I began my search for them in all the usual places. The more I looked for them, the more anxious I became. I had a clear focus, but not a focus that felt good. I wanted my sunglasses back, sure, but the driving force behind my actions was that I did NOT want to spend another $200 on sunglasses.

I searched every drawer in the house. Tousled all the couch cushions. I walked an acre of our property (twice), reasoning that they might have fallen off my hat while gardening. Nothing.

It was too late to keep searching, so I gave up for the night. In the morning, I remembered that I'd been to a couple local stores the last day I remembered having the glasses. I drove to them and while people were very nice to me, no, no one had turned in any sunglasses.

As I drove home, I felt my thoughts shifting.

Okay, I thought. *I give up.*

I've looked EVERYWHERE. And they're just gone.

Maybe the'll show up in one of those crazy places some day when I least expect it.

I can wear my old pair for a while.

I can afford a new pair.

This is really not a big deal.

Within a few minutes, I returned to my house. When I walked through the door, I felt the inspiration to check our storage bureau where I usually leave my sunglasses. I opened the first drawer, and nothing. Then I moved to my wife's drawer (separate drawers = happy marriage), and what do you know? My sunglasses. I'd checked in this very drawer an hour earlier, and I could not see them. I'd missed them the previous day, too.

Now let's think about this for a minute, because we're talking about more than sunglasses.

The sunglasses were there the whole time. But **I literally could not see them**. When I opened the drawer previously, I operated from the wavelength of "My glasses are lost! Shit! I really DON'T want to spend another $200. I can't believe I was so careless to lose them."

Back to the metaphysics for a moment, my original search was rooted in resistance. My actions were guided by everything I didn't want to be experiencing. And from this place, I was choosing to live in a completely separate dimension from the one in which my desire existed. When you're not a vibrational match for your desires, you cannot see them. You cannot experience them. All of your desires exist (we could be talking about sunglasses, awesome relationships, or a fat bank account), but when you're not a match, they remain on a separate plane, just outside the realm of your awareness. This is why I could not see the glasses until I relaxed. (I've replicated this phenomenon many times with things I've misplaced. So have you, right?)

In order to be a match to having what you want, laying down your resistance is very often the most powerful thing you can do. In this example I directed my thoughts to the place where I was willing *not* to have what I wanted. I said to myself, *They're gone. That sucks, but, oh well... I'll get another pair. Hell, maybe I'll get a different model this time.*

At first this might seem counter-intuitive, especially given our culture's reverence for dogged persistence, never giving up, and the necessity to push yourself to get what you want. But when pushing forward and being propelled by thoughts of what you DON'T want, you're introducing a tremendous amount of resistance into the equation. You can't focus on what you DON'T want and experience what you DO want. This is just math.

So, if you will allow yourself to get to the place where you're willing NOT to have your desires, guess what? You stop pushing against what you DON'T want. You stop approaching your desires from the place of need. Once you're willing to NOT have your desire, the iron curtain of resistance you've been holding falls to the floor. And when the curtain falls, your desire is waiting for you on the other side. The thing you've been wanting, the thing to which you've been blind, now becomes completely obvious.

For clarity's sake, it's worth going a bit deeper on what I mean by "being willing NOT to have your desires." If you're pissed about not having something you want, vibrationally you're living in the energy of neediness. Neediness is never attractive.

If you want an easy way to think about the repulsive nature of need-based energy, look to relationships. Think to a needy person in your experience, someone who *needs* something from you (your love, your attention, your money). Now ask yourself whether this energy is attractive or repulsive?

Need is always based on a belief of scarcity, that's there's not enough to go around, so every morsel must be clung to. That clinging energy feels draining because your inner being knows that the Universe is infinitely abundant. Thoughts of scarcity will never resonate with your inner being and so they will always feel bad to you.

When you need something, you're just asserting that you don't have it. When you assert you don't have something, the Law of the Universe works tirelessly to fulfill your assertion. When you assert that you don't have something that you want, you will always be proven correct.

Back to my example, when I became willing to *not* find my lost glasses, I accepted the present moment as okay. No, I certainly didn't like this idea, but the key was that I stopped fighting and dropped my resistance against the outcome I did not want. When I freed myself of any whiff of neediness, I freed myself up to rendezvous with my desire again.

Simply put, one of the fastest ways to get what you want is to let it go by saying, *"I don't need it. I'm willing NOT to have it."*

Here's some specific areas to consider where you might want to shift to a willingness to NOT have your desire...

If you want more money in your account, are you willing to have zero dollars?

If you want a great relationship, are you willing to be alone forever?

If you want to be successful in ways that are meaningful to you, are you willing to fail in ways that are meaningful to you?

If you want to live by following your own intuition, are you willing to be seen as foolish, lazy, or irresponsible by other people?

Simply put, no matter the subject, if you can practice directing your thoughts to the point where you can say, "I don't like the thought of not having [it], but I don't need it. I'm willing to let it go...," you've just put yourself on the trail to having what you want.

IT'S GOING TO GET BETTER
FROM HERE

YESTERDAY I HAD one of those days I would not choose to repeat.

I did not sleep well. Early in the morning, I got angry with my son (he pissed on the carpet, twice, just like the thug in *The Big Lebowski*). I felt resentful toward my wife. The new dishwasher went on the fritz. Nothing was going the way I wanted it to. With every thing that went wrong, I just got more and more upset.

My dominant thought was "Everything is fucked up!"

There's a lot of power behind a thought like that. And there's a lot of momentum (in an unwanted direction) behind this thought. Even though I was fully aware that I was out of alignment, I could not stop myself. The train was moving too fast. I couldn't just quit, couldn't let it go. I couldn't just bring myself to go inside, grab a beer, and watch some baseball.

Instead, I pushed forward. Acting from what I did NOT want (I did not want to be "unproductive" for the whole day), I got the bright idea to spray a second coat of stain on my shed. After

44

setting up for half an hour, and opening a fresh can of stain, I got started. I sprayed a few strokes on the side of the shed before I noticed it. The young man at the hardware store mixed the new can of stain improperly; it didn't match the first coat. Now I had to clean the paint sprayer (another 30 minutes) and would eventually have to return to the store and start all over.

For a moment, I wanted to cry. The day was a disaster. I'd ignored my feelings all day and tried to bust through the powerful feelings of resistance that I set in motion to start the day. But now, I'd hit my threshold. I decided to give up. I put away my tools. I went inside and moped on the couch.

I reached for a better feeling thought, something to release the pressure I'd put on myself.

"This too shall pass... This is all temporary," is what came out.

And I felt a little better. Notice I did not say I felt good. However, by allowing myself to have a shitty day, I felt a *little* better. I was no longer resisting my current reality. From this place I was able to get a step farther by allowing myself to be okay with the fact that I had created this shitty day. In other words, I stopped beating myself up for what I'd created. I allowed myself to feel the relief from the letting go of pushing so hard.

When you find yourself focused on something you don't like (static in a relationship, a smaller number in your bank account than you'd like, etc.) saying This Too Shall Pass can be very powerful because you are no longer trying to push away something you created and don't like.

In effect, you're saying, yes, this is the current reality. And no, I don't particularly like it, but things will change soon because I am deciding what it is that I want from here.

When you say This Too Shall Pass, you begin the process of asserting that things will be getting better in short order while simultaneously letting yourself off the hook. By making this very powerful decision, you unkink your hose of well-being. You will feel the sense of relief immediately as you tune into the feeling of allowing once again.

Whatever's going on in your life right now is all temporary as everything is wanting to change, evolve, and expand. When you bump into something you don't like and you fixate on it, you stop the flow and evolution of things. Instead of allowing the unwanted experience to move on from you and evolve, dwelling on something you don't like only causes it to expand. The good news is that the problem will grow in intensity until you can no longer bear the weight of the resistance and give up.

While you don't have to let things get to such an uncomfortable point if you give up early, should you continue pressing on until you hit the wall, just remember these four words: *This Too Shall Pass*. Notice the feeling of relief. It is your clear signal that you've dropped your resistance and resumed your natural state of allowing. Anything and everything unwanted is temporary when you allow yourself to let it go and drop your resistance to its presence.

STOP RESISTING YOUR OWN THOUGHTS

❦

IF YOU REALLY WANT TO ALLOW YOUR desires to flow into your experience easily (and who doesn't?), you'll want to give up the subtle (and often hidden) habit of resisting your own thoughts. Right now, I'll bet that you're doing this much more than you're currently aware, so applying the power of letting go in this area has the potential to bust your life wide open.

First, let's explore a couple questions to clarify what this really means. *What does it mean to resist your own thoughts? Why would you ever do this?*

Resisting your thoughts is the insidious habit of making the judgment that some of your thoughts are not okay. Somewhere along the line, you've taken on the idea that some of your thoughts are good and some are bad. Good thoughts would be those aligned with love, appreciation or fun and bad thoughts would be fear, jealousy, judgment, disappointment, or anger.

But here's the thing: Just like there are no bad clouds in the sky, there are no bad thoughts. Just as some clouds are puffy, light, and white, others are dark, heavy and full of rain. But every

47

cloud is worthwhile and serves a purpose. The same is true for your thoughts. Every one of your thoughts — even the ones you don't particularly like — are there for your benefit.

For example, jealousy tells you that you are seeing someone else experiencing something that you want, something you don't believe you can have. This is powerful information. Jealousy shines a light directly on an unwanted belief you probably want to drop. It's here to serve you.

However, we're taught that some thoughts are unacceptable, impolite, or even dangerous. We're taught it's not nice to be jealous. You're not supposed to feel angry. But there's a world of difference between thinking a negative thought and dwelling there. Having unwanted thoughts provides the launching pad for every one of your desires. Consider that at one point, early on in your life, you noticed that you did not like to be stuck in one spot when all these bigger people around you were moving around freely. Your dissatisfaction with being immobile launched your desire to walk. Just look at you now!

(Ironically, this fear-of-negative-thoughts myth has been perpetuated by many teachers in the personal development/Law of Attraction realm. Now we can put it to bed. In a word, it's bullshit. There are no bad thoughts that you need to fear.)

It's worth noting that some fearful thoughts can be uncomfortable. So instead of allowing these thoughts and being present with them for a moment, you likely scoop them up and stuff them in the nearest closet, and then do your best to pretend they do not exist.

However, true allowing (the real endgame of letting go), requires you to allow the thought that you DON'T like in addition to the ones you do. The metaphysics to support this are very clear. When you allow your thoughts, they move through you like passing clouds in the sky. And when you try to resist thoughts you don't like, those thoughts hang around like dirty laundry.

So how do you know where you're resisting some thoughts in your life? Simple. Focus on some desire that you have that's not yet manifested. Somewhere in there, there's a thought you're resisting.

True allowing is allowing the thought that you DON'T like.

You did not come into this life to like everything or everyone. You did not come into this life to walk through it free of opinions and preferences.

When you look at something you don't particularly like, such as a bank account with a low balance, your job is not to submissively think, "Whatever…"

For years when I'd look at my bank account and see how little money I had, my initial reaction was to resent the fact that I didn't have more. I resented people (people I didn't even know) for having more. I felt so angry I wanted to throw things. But I didn't. I didn't allow myself to feel pissed off. I didn't allow myself to think my angry thoughts because somewhere down the line I was taught to avoid these thoughts and that I should just be grateful for what I had. I'd learned that being jealous wasn't *spiritual*. As a result of eating my anger, well, nothing much changed in my bank account. There was always enough, but never much more than enough.

Then I allowed myself to let go and stop resisting my thoughts. I stared at my balance on the screen and just allowed myself to get royally pissed off. I finally stopped pretending that I was okay with my money situation, when deeper down I clearly was not. I wanted more, dammit!

So, I let my thoughts just run wild for a few minutes. I let them take me to whatever ridiculous place they wanted to go. I allowed myself to think how unfair all of this was. I allowed myself to feel my fear of not having enough. I allowed myself to think what it would feel like to punch those rich assholes in the teeth... and so on. By allowing these thoughts that I did not like to come out, I finally allowed myself to stand in the clarity of my desire.

I am ready to have more money.

STOP RESISTING YOUR THOUGHTS
ABOUT OTHER PEOPLE

MY SON IS about to turn 3. He knows what he wants, he knows what he likes and he states his preferences with no trace of hesitation.

On two occasions, he's walked up to a guest in our home and stated, "I don't like you!" without a trace of remorse.

Of course, this could be a source of embarrassment for a parent. We want our kids to be polite and say nice things to other people. In fact, we usually prefer them to "be nice" rather than express their true feelings.

My first reaction was to want to say, "Alex, we don't talk like that to other people!" But I caught myself and didn't make any comment or try to correct him. He was just being himself, and you know what? I realized I agreed with him. In both cases, I did not really like either person, either, so why would I teach my child to discount his feelings, especially given their awesome power to guide us through life?

Now, I have several years left to break my son's spirit and teach him what so many well-meaning parents and teachers taught most of us: *Be a good boy. Be a good girl. Get along with everyone. Good boys and girls don't think bad thoughts about other people.*

We allow these thoughts about what it means to be a good person to take root as we mature into adulthood. In short, the resulting belief is something like *Good people don't think bad thoughts. Especially toward other people.* This is especially true in the realm of personal development, by the way. Most every speaker or book in the genre tells you keep your thoughts positive, all the time, no matter the subject. Find the good in everyone.

While this makes sense given what you've been taught, it's total nonsense. As you move through your life, you're not going to like some things. You're *really* not going to like some people. And that's perfectly A-OK. That's exactly as it should be.

The real problem comes when you try to stifle some thought or feeling that society has taught you to believe isn't polite or appropriate. When this happens (and it's likely that you do this much more than you are currently aware), you're resisting your own thoughts and feelings. And guess what? Resisting anything, even your own harsh thoughts about someone, causes those thoughts to lodge themselves deeper in your mind. Once entrenched, like a virus, they grow bigger and fester. Not allowing yourself to feel what you feel is a version of an auto-immune disease.

You don't want any part of that. Let it go.

BE WILLING

REMEMBER that the real key to your desire is to ALLOW your desire.

Just stop pushing. Get out of the way. And allow.

So here's a simple idea that will swing your "Allowing Door" wide open.

Be *Willing*.

If you want to be wealthy, you must *be willing* to be poor.

If you want to a lean body, you must *be willing* to be fat.

If you want to be in a great relationship, you must *be willing* to be alone.

If you want feel healthy, you must *be willing* to feel sick.

If you want to be successful, you must *be willing* to fail.

At first glance, this may not make sense. Wouldn't a willingness to fail open the door to creating failure?

No.

And here's why…

If you're not willing, you're resisting.

Consider that most of your desires are likely not very pure desires. In other words, if you have a desire that's not yet manifested, it's very likely because you are more focused on WHAT YOU DON'T WANT than you are focused on the pleasure of having your desire.

For example, if you ask people what they really want, one of the most common answers is more money. Now, when you take things a step further and ask these folks why they want more money, they usually offer something akin to "well, then I could pay off all my bills" or "then I wouldn't feel so worried all the time."

In other words the desire is rooted in NOT wanting to feel poor. When this is the case, metaphorically speaking, you will always be doing battle with the Poor Monster, fighting to keep him at arm's length so you can avoid having to sleep under a bridge somewhere in the cold.

When you close the door to keep what you DON'T want *out* of your life, you're also blocking the path for your desires to come *in*. Sure, if you're not willing to be poor, enough money will be able to slip through the cracks around the door and allow you enough to get by, but you'll never experience the full, free flow of money that you really desire, either. For that to happen, you've got to open the door of allowing completely.

So how do you open the door and keep from blocking the entranceway?

Decide to become willing.

In willingness, you drop the resistance and fear to experiencing what you don't want. When you embrace your vulnerability through willingness, you unlock the gateway and now the wanted stuff can come in.

Now, let me be clear here. Sticking with the example of money, just because you're willing to be poor does not mean that you want to be poor or even that you remotely like the idea of being poor. Of course you don't. But the key here is that you can not like something, let the thought be what it is, and just put your focus elsewhere instead of pushing up against the thought out of fear.

Here's a simple example of not pushing against what you don't like. I don't like olives. My wife and kids love them. Even though I don't like them, I am willing to have them in my house. I don't yell at my wife for having them in the refrigerator. I just ignore them and I don't eat them. Simple. However, if every time I saw my family eating olives, I pushed against them, perhaps saying something like, "I can't believe you are eating those disgusting things!" it would come as no surprise if the next time I ordered a pizza, a few stray olives found their way to my pie. Simply put, when you find yourself creating unwanted outcomes (big or small), this is your clear feedback that you're pushing against something you don't want and it's time to become willing. I don't like olives and I doubt I ever will. But if one lands on my plate, I am willing to just flick it off, and so I have few unwanted olive encounters these days.

As a final point on being willing, it's important to note that you can't bullshit yourself here. This isn't about saying you're willing if you don't really mean it. Remember, we live in a vibrational universe, and so the universe operates only on vibration, not words. So to be willing, you need to really let go and feel the relief of dropping your resistance to potential unwanted outcomes. After all, the relief is what you're really looking for anyway.

To tune into this feeling, just take a few minutes on a couch to imagine yourself experiencing whatever you're fighting so hard against. Imagine that bank account on the screen at zero. Imagine that scale forever stuck on that number you think is too high. Imagine those people laughing at you self-righteously because you thought you could live your life differently from them. Imagine yourself alone forever.

When you're willing to think these thoughts, to look them in the eye and let them be what they are, you'll see how quickly they evolve away from you, like morning dew evaporating on a hot summer day. When you're willing NOT to have your desire, you are open to *allowing* it into your life.

A KING COMMANDS

Okay, I know I just told you to be willing NOT to have something, and here I am telling you to Have What You Want and To Have it Right Now.

In one breath, I'm saying you're better served being willing to not having your desires, and in the next I'm saying take a stand for them.

Don't those things contradict?

No. No they don't.

And here's why...

Remember that what we're really talking about is dropping any forms of resistance, because when you drop resistance, you enter the state of Allowing.

When you want something, but don't *need* it, you drop the resistance that accompanies need.

Now I am suggesting a completely different route to your

desires, the path of certainty. Stand behind what you want. Want it because you want it. No rationalizing. Have it just because you decide to have it. And have it NOW!

Practice commanding your desires with the certainty of a king or queen. Think about it. A king does not ask. Or hope. Or wish... *A king commands.* A king does not doubt whether his underlings will follow his orders.

Notice that whatever your desire, when you are certain of it coming into your life, it manifests. And no, there are no exceptions to this rule. If you find yourself saying, "No Drew, you're wrong. There are things I want very badly and they never seem to come into my life," this tells me that somewhere in the mix, you have some doubt or hesitation regarding your desire. In this case, now would be a good time for you to apply whichever principle from this book that feels best to you in the moment.

You can think about it this way: Have you ever decided that you were going to find the perfect parking space in a crowded lot — that despite the logical odds, all the other cars, all the other drivers hunting for that same spot — that YOU would be the one to get it? Sure you have. And when you do, you get to enjoy that delicious moment of triumph when another car leaves, opening up your spot at just the perfect time. How sweet, right? Certainly this feels magical, and your passenger might call you lucky, but deep down you knew you had it all the way. You were certain in your desire, even when there was no evidence that it could be fulfilled, and so it manifests. If you can take that same level of expectation and certainty to any and all of your other desires, they are yours. Whether it's a parking space or a vacation home on the ocean, when you assert it's yours, it is.

Of course, the sticking point arises when you start entertaining the *But Hows.* As in, "I want a new house, lover, pile of money... *But How* is this going to happen?"

When you ask yourself this question, the answer is always the same. The answer is always *I don't know*. And when you take a moment to notice how *I don't know* feels, it always feels bad. The decision to keep your focus on the But Hows creates the resistance that keeps you from realizing those desires.

Focusing on the But Hows is silly. You don't ask how your cell phone works. Or the Internet. Or electricity. You don't know how a seed becomes a plant. Or how you originated from a few cells. Truth is, you don't care how these things work. You expect them to work. They do.

The same holds for your desires.

Allow yourself to say, I'll have it NOW. Don't wait a minute longer. Command your desire with the presence of royalty and allow the universe to orchestrate the details. Take ten minutes to sit quietly and imagine having your desire now.

Feel it NOW because imagining is the work of all creation. The practice of being in alignment with your desires NOW, instead of a time when you figure it all out (a time that never comes, but the way), is all that's required. So stop waiting. Immerse yourself in that wonderful feeling of certainty.

When doubts arise and you find yourself saying, "I'm imagining, but I don't *really* have it," make a new decision. Say to yourself, *But I do. I do have it. I am right in the middle of my heart's desire and I can feel it. It's here.* Reconnect to the feeling of your desire's presence in your life.

In short, it's time to become a certain SOB regarding your desires. No hoping. No compromising your desires for what you think you can get instead of what you really want.

When you live in the certainty of having what you really want, when you let go of the questions and the doubts, it's yours. That's the rule. There are no exceptions.

DARE TO FAIL

A WILLINGNESS TO FAIL? If that sounds like a really dumb idea, I get it. Believe me, as much as I'm wired to say *fuck it* in my life, when it came down to being willing to fail, I resisted.

Me fail? No way, no how.

For most of my life, I avoided failure at all costs. It was not until I began writing this that I began to clearly see and feel all the ways that my unwillingness to fail locked me in limbo.

Ironically, I learned to fear failing in school. Throughout my education, my fellow students and I were graded, ranked, and sorted into herds. Education was a competition in which metrics and standards were used to separate the winners from the losers. Certainly, every child was aware of his or her place in the pecking order.

The students who failed to measure up were viewed as problems in need of fixing. Those administrators of the system never interpreted your failure as meaning your interests and aptitudes lay elsewhere. Failure was never interpreted to mean that the test was bogus. No, failure not only meant that you

were doing something wrong, **failure meant there was something wrong with YOU**.

Looking back upon the powerful messages of our formative
years regarding failure, an unwillingness to fail seems quite a
reasonable tactic both for survival and as a strategy for getting
ahead. I know that I took on a strong belief that failing at something would be about the worst thing that could happen. I
worked diligently to avoid such an outcome in all areas of my
life, from my relationships to my business to my finances.

Note: an unwillingness to fail has a similar energetic vibration
as a fear of failure. Like anything that you resist, when you're
trying to push something away, it sticks around like a party
guest who cannot take a hint. An unwillingness to fail delays the
manifestation of your desire.

After I got married and the children arrived, my income
declined for a few successive years. While I did not like it, this is
what I told myself: Things would turn around as my free time
returned.

But here's what really happened...

As I took on more responsibilities, I became less willing to fail.
This seems like a very practical thing to do. After all, I have to
provide for my family. It's not just me any more. This is serious
business. We don't want to screw things up and end up living in
a lean-to.

With so much responsibility for little lives, failure was not an
option. From a traditional way of thinking, playing things safe
seemed to make tremendous practical sense. But when it comes
to our desires, playing things safe is often the riskiest thing we
can do. It plays out in sports: One team has a lead as time starts
winding down and starts playing not to lose instead of
executing with the passion that captured the lead. You can feel

the energy through the TV screen. The team that's playing not to lose tenses up. A single play shifts the energy to the opponent and you witness an incredible comeback/incredible choke job. Look deeper and you'll see just another example where the fear of failing creates an unwanted outcome.

Going back to my life, my intuition was telling me it was time to shake up the structure of my coaching practice. I wanted to change how and when I was available to my clients in ways that were more pleasing to me. But even though I clearly knew what felt better to me, the thoughts of failure mushroomed up from the soil.

Those thoughts flowed something like this...

What if my current clients don't like the changes and decide to leave?

If I lose clients, my income will plummet.

If my income plummets, will I be able to pay the mortgage?

And so on...

My focus on not failing lingered for a couple of years. I knew I wanted to make these changes, but I continued to push my intuition aside and hold myself back from my desire.

Over time all of my clients went away. My income stagnated. I frequently entertained all the torturous thoughts about not having enough money.

This was the direct result of my not being willing to let go and fail. Just like being a kid in school, I did not want other people to see me a loser. Even though I'd been a successful coach for more than a decade, I still secretly feared the thought of people pointing at me and saying, See what happens when you're a lazy dreamer?

When those thoughts came up, instead letting them wash over

me, I tried to make them go away by doing something. I'd send out an e-mail to my list, I'd start creating a new program. All of this made sense when you listen to marketers and business coaches, but because my actions were rooted in the fear of an unwillingness to fail, they had no chance to provide the results I wanted. My fear drove my actions enough times that I finally gave up.

When I realized I needed to be willing to entertain failure, I went to my office and looked in the mirror. An answer came to me: my big fear was that somehow I would lose my house. I was so afraid of the thought, so unwilling to even entertain it, that all of my energy was focused on keeping it away from me. As a result, it hung around and haunted me.

Allowing myself to connect to the thought of failing and losing my house went something like this...

(Failure thought) Okay, so what would it really be like if I screwed the pooch and lost the house?

(Pause)

Well, we'd be okay. Somehow, someway, we'd manage.

I've lived in lots of apartments before. And, really, they were fine.

I've always found a way. And I always will find a way.

I have hundreds of thousands of dollars of credit.

I actually have enough money in various retirement accounts to pay off the mortgage if I wanted to.

I don't need to worry about losing the house. That's just kind of silly.

I wonder what's for dinner?

Here's the takeaway of this simple example. By taking ten minutes to allow myself to let go enough to entertain my deepest fear of failing, I stopped resisting it. When I stopped resisting the fearful thought, I allowed it to start evolving away from me. The mere willingness to sit with thoughts of failure caused it to fade. I immediately felt a deep sense of relief.

Shortly thereafter, I made the changes I wanted to make within my business and allowed the clients and dollars to flow more easily than ever before. Turns out, (as it always does), I was the only thing in the way.

Over the years I've been witness to the stranglehold that an unwillingness to fail or to "do it wrong" has on people. I've seen it keep people from ever getting into a relationship. (*Too risky. Might fail.*) I've seen it keep people suffering in the wrong relationships for decades. (*Only losers get divorced.*) But most disheartening, I've seen it keep lots of people living small, never daring to mash their creative stamp on the world.

Failure is not an indictment of you being a lesser person in some way. It's an indicator that you're simply not in alignment with something. Take a moment to consider that **all the things you really like in your life are the direct result of some previous failure**.

For example, for every failed relationship you were part of, you left the relationship with more clarity of what you wanted your next partner to be like. Without the contrast of failure, new desires cannot be born. Failure is the helpful feedback that shows you what it is that you're *really wanting now*, right in this moment.

You will be failing in all sorts of ways for the rest of your life. Make mistakes as fast as you can. Drop your resistance to thoughts of failing and you open yourself to thriving.

KEEP IT SIMPLE

THE REAL KEY underlying the manifestation of all of your desires is alignment. When you are aligned with your desires (you expect them, you anticipate them, you bask in the "having of your desires NOW"), you let go of any potential resistance. When this happens, the stuff you want shows up in your life.

So here's the thing... Do you know how alignment feels? Of course you do. Certainly it feels good. It feels easy. It feels like being in the flow of life.

Another way of saying this is that alignment feels *simple*. More specifically, alignment feels *simple to you*.

When I entered college, the people who'd guided me in high school convinced me that I should become an engineer ("the world's always going to need engineers!") even though my aptitudes and interests lay elsewhere. I took the advice of my well-meaning elders and found myself sitting in a calculus class during freshman year. Now, my university designed calculus to be extra hard, a weeder class for the engineer wannabes so that 40% of the students failed every semester.

Terrified of failing, I studied for two hours every night just to cling. A couple friends got A's without studying. They could "see" calculus. To me, calculus was a foreign language.

The A students were aligned with becoming scientists, mathematicians, and engineers. That's why the work was so simple for them. But I had no interest in this field of study or this way of thinking. I was just following the advice of people I assumed knew what was best for me. I dreaded the classes and the tests so much that I still wake up with the occasional test-anxiety nightmare.

My sophomore year I took some electives. On the first day of my first psychology class, I knew this was where I belonged. I still had to study, but studying felt like expansion, not drudgery. I looked forward to going to classes. I thrived. Looking back, following what felt simple and obvious to me changed the entire course of my life. (I still love what I do every day.)

Now to be clear, it's worth noting that there's a distinction between something feeling simple (aligned) to you and something being free of effort. Certainly, I had to study quite hard in my psychology classes, but most of the time, I really loved what I was learning, whereas studying calculus was hard labor.

Here's the point: If it feels simple and obvious, it's for you. You're aligned with it.

If it does not feel simple and clear to you, let it go. Give up. It's not for you. You're not aligned with it. And most important, **you don't need to try to align yourself with anything that does not feel simple to you**. You are free to try, of course, but this approach is full of resistance and never really works out very well.

Giving up the complex ideas of who you "should be" and what you "should do" and embracing only the things in life that feel simple and obvious for you is one of the most liberating things you can do. But it really requires the courage of saying no to those old beliefs, usually those ideas that look good, *but do not feel good.*

When I announced I was dropping out of engineering to major in psychology, my decision was not met with much enthusiasm.

"What are you going to do with that degree?" was the common refrain. While I didn't have an answer, I allowed myself the freedom of not knowing or caring. Going with what felt simple and aligned just felt too good. Looking back, taking the path that felt simple and obvious has made my life simpler in too many ways to count.

To leverage the power of keeping it simple, apply this key to your everyday life decisions. Even with the small stuff, because there really is no small stuff. Everything you do brings momentum that will expand.

As someone trained to be a problem-solver, I like to keep in mind that just because you *could* figure something out and solve the problem, doesn't mean that you must. When some problem stops feeling simple, leave it alone for a while. Don't be surprised when the problem gets solved for you (this happens to me all the time with my computer issues).

Play with this. See what happens when you walk through your life today asserting that *If it's not simple, it's not for me* and letting go of anything you are pushing against. You'll know you're making progress when you drop something that feels complex and then shortly after you get some clear evidence reminding you how the Universe is always working on your behalf.

BE VULNERABLE

I REMEMBER SEEING this phenomenon play out during a memorable moment of my life. In order to earn a Ph.D in psychology, I was required to go through a number of *defenses* (that's what they're really called) in front of a small committee. Imagine being in a small room with six professors who believe it's their job to put you on trial. They grill you as to why you made certain research decisions, or chose one statistical analysis over another, and so on. As a candidate, your job is to defend yourself against questions that are attacks on your work.

In the life of a grad student, there was no more important (or stressful) day than a defense day. After a defense, fellow students would all meet for drinks and compare notes about their experiences. Stories of three or four intolerable hours arguing for ideas and methodology were common. Many of us failed the first time around.

I'd listened to enough stories to recognize a pattern. The more defending, the worse the defense went. On the surface this might seem counter-intuitive. But professors tend to have big egos; they won't let a student win an argument, especially in front of their colleagues. So the more you approached a defense in a defensive posture and fought for your ideas, the greater the likelihood that the room would witness a pissing contest — and a contest that the student was going to lose. In this case, losing meant months of extra work doing revisions and then having to stand trial once again.

By the time I got to my dissertation defense, I just wanted to be done with the whole graduate school experience. My intention was clear: My defense would be *easy*. I would walk out of the room having been awarded my degree with no revisions and that would be that. To manifest this intention, I made the radical decision to make myself defenseless.

More specifically, when the statistics professor challenged me as to why I didn't do some obscure analysis only he cared about, I didn't come back defending the analysis that I had chosen to do. Instead, I calmly told him I hadn't thought of his approach and that I could see the merits of his idea. Likewise, when other challenges came, I'd simply agree with the criticism directed at me and allow silence to fill the room.

So while they threw their jabs at me, I remained true to my decision to be vulnerable and allowed let them hit me without fighting back. In fact, my strategy was not unlike Jesus' advice when he said to "turn the other cheek" ("But I tell you, Do not resist an evil person. If someone strikes you on the right cheek, turn to him the other also" Matthew 5:39).

Turning the other cheek is not about pacifism or being a martyr, it's about letting unwanted events go through non-resistance. In this example, because I never punched back, there was never a spark of tension in the room. There was no momentum for conflict.

Exactly one hour after my defense began, the committee

members sent me out of the conference room to talk over my fate. My friend Mary, the office secretary, called me over, alarmed. Why wasn't I still in the meeting room, she asked? When I told her the defense was over, she shared that in her 30 years in the office she'd never seen a dissertation defense shorter than two hours and here I was done in half that time.

In the next moment, the chairman then called me back into the room and said, "Congratulations, Dr. Rozell. You've passed with no revisions necessary."

When we approach a situation with our fists up, we can expect a fight. While there's nothing wrong with a fight (some people love to operate this way), if you're interested in getting what you want with ease and without the stress of battle, dropping your defenses is an overlooked strategy.

Start experimenting with what happens when you allow yourself to be vulnerable. The next time you argue with a loved one, see what happens when you let the other person win. The next time you feel the impulse to defend one of your beliefs, see what happens when you choose not to.

While dropping your defenses applies to your interactions with other people, experiment with dropping your defenses toward yourself as well.

Right now it's likely that you have lots of judgmental thoughts toward yourself. These thoughts may have something to do with your appearance, your level of success, whether you're a good person, doing the right things, etc. If you have a thought about yourself that you don't like and it's been hanging around for some time, you are defending yourself against this thought. You're trying to rationalize it, or pretend it's not there, or just hide from it. If this is the case, you know that none of these strategies work, because you're just resisting your thought. As long as you're defending yourself from a thought you don't like, it will stay with you.

Every thought you have, even the dark, judgmental ones about other people or yourself, wants to be *thunk*. That is, the thought wants to be allowed to exist. When you allow your thoughts, they evolve and move on from you. (This is one of the most freeing things you can do for yourself, so I highly encourage you to look at the thoughts you're resisting.)

If in the back of your mind you think you're a loser (or whatever), then let take a couple minutes to bring that thought out into the light. Judge the hell out of yourself. Be defenseless toward this unwanted thought. When you do this, in no time at all, you'll see your thought evolve. You'll likely think it silly and irrelevant. As a result, you'll be free of this thought toward yourself and you'll feel the relief immediately.

This concept can be applied to just about any situation where you feel stuck or to a subject where you've felt frustrated for a long time. Instead of fighting and pushing harder, take the opposite approach. Lay your arms down. Raise your hands in the air. Surrender to the person or the thought. Let it go. Be courageous enough to turn the other cheek.

When you do, you'll be amazed how quickly the fighting gets replaced with peace.

EMBRACE THE S WORD

THE KEY to letting go and allowing your desires is to live in the state of alignment. When you're aligned and feeling good, you are an allower.

This sounds simple, right? Because it is simple.

However, there is a catch. In order to consistently feel good, you'll need to care about your own alignment first. You need to be selfish.

Selfish.

Uh Oh...

Selfish...

Most people would rather swallow a live beetle than embrace the word. After all, you were likely taught that there are few things more worthy of scorn than being selfish. But understand that in this context of this word, being selfish is really about paying attention to the answer of the question, *What feels better to me?*

Being selfish is not about willfully trying to neglect, to manipulate, or to be excluding of others. In fact, despite what you've learned, being selfish has nothing whatsoever to do with other people. Being selfish has everything thing to do with you and your connection to your inner being, who you really are. Being selfish means being self-oriented in that you are choosing to live in alignment with YOU.

Look around (and perhaps within) and you'll notice how people are terrified of following their own bliss because they fear what someone else will think. If the thought of being selfish brings up a visceral reaction, it's likely that you were taught not to be selfish by someone who wanted you to behave in manner that matched *their* preferences.

The underlying message is You shouldn't be following what makes YOU happy, you should be doing what makes ME happy — the most perfectly ironic example of the selfish behavior they warned you about. Oscar Wilde said it best: "Selfishness is not living as one wishes to live, it is asking others to live as one wishes to live."

Keep in mind that if you're truly wanting to help those around you and you're not willing to be selfish enough to follow your own path of alignment, then you really have very little to offer. A common example is the miserable married couple who stay together because they don't want to be selfish regarding the kids. In their selflessness, this couple teaches their children that marriage is supposed to be a miserable grind. So let's be very clear, here. When you take on the role of the martyr, you leave yourself with little to contribute to the well-being of those around you. However, when you're selfishly following what feels better to you and allowing yourself to be happy, all those who come into your presence are positively impacted by the experience of being near you.

So if you want your life to be easy, if you want to feel your true power as the creator of all you experience, if you want to simply allow your desires in your life, you'll need to be selfish enough to turn inward and feel where your alignment lies, and then have the courage to follow what feels better.

No, this is not always the easy choice in a culture that has its own selfish agenda for how you should behave. But to continue Wilde's quote, "A red rose is not selfish because it wants to be a red rose."

Whatever your desire, it's perfect. Because it's yours. The only real question around whatever desire you have is not whether it's valid, worthy, or doable, but rather will you allow yourself to have it?

In order to be that allower of your desires, if you're not selfish enough to make feeling good your first priority, you simply won't be able to align with the energy of your higher self, because your higher self always feels good.

The threat of being called selfish was a powerful weapon used to manipulate you when you were seven. If you want to allow your desires, you're going to have to be selfish enough to let go of the opinions and preferences of others. You're going to have to start listening to how you feel and choose the paths that YOU prefer.

THE RIGHT THING AIN'T ALWAYS

Okay, let's get this straight, right now.

There is no *right* thing to do.

There's what feels better for you to do, and what feels worse for you to do.

That's it.

This is worth remembering because the idea of doing the right thing dictates many of your actions and decisions, most of which fly under your awareness. And the catch is that these actions and decisions, while looking right on the surface of things, are really driven by the fear of doing the wrong thing or being seen as selfish. When you're doing things to avoid being seen in a negative light, you're in a state of resistance. And as you know by now, where there is resistance, things tend to get messy, fast.

As a personal example, I think back to visiting my mom in a nursing home years ago. She had Alzheimer's. The experience of seeing her never failed to depress me. Certainly, visiting her regularly was the *right* thing to do. After all, she and I were very close and she only lived a few miles down the road. And did I mention she was my Mom? I mean, what kind of selfish asshole would I be if I stopped seeing her? Well, it turns out, the happy kind.

I never felt better after visiting my mom and my funky mood would linger. The visits affected me enough where I sat myself down and asked myself why I kept going back to the nursing home when none of my experiences were pleasant. The answer came quickly.

I'd feel guilty if I didn't go.

Now the thoughts surrounding guilt, while able to elicit powerful reactions, are really bullshit. The bad feeling associated with guilt is not telling you that you're doing anything wrong. That bad feeling is your indicator that your thoughts about the situation are out of whack with how your Aligned Self sees things. When I understood this distinction, I decided to stop seeing my mom. I would visit whenever it felt better for me to do so.

I did not visit my mom often in the last year or two of her life. I can't speak for my mom, but in my heart I don't believe she missed me. What I know for sure is that letting go of this burden of doing the right thing lifted a massive weight from my being. I experienced the freedom and lightness of leaving guilt behind on the old, dusty trail and I've been much more aware of the fact that picking it up is always optional.

It's worth repeating that there is no objective *right* thing to do, ever. Let that belief go. There's what feels better to you and what feels worse. What's right for you is what's right for YOU and you discern this by using your inner GPS and simply noticing what FEELS better to you. Not what LOOKS better...

Not what your mom thought was the right thing to do... Not what you think will keep you safe from your own judgments about yourself...

Noticing what feels better to you and following that path requires you to be selfish enough to make how you feel your priority because you understand that all the good that comes in your life depends on you feeling good. This takes awareness, courage, and practice because you're probably used to doing so many things because they look right. But in order to relax your way into your desires, you're going to have to let go of lots of old patterns of behavior.

So before you say YES to something, no matter how good, smart, or right it may seem on the face of things, take a beat to go inward and see if saying YES feels like a "Hell, YES!"

If it doesn't, that's your Aligned Self telling you this is really not the right thing for you.

Allow yourself to say No to doing the "right" thing.

TAKE A NAP

When the going gets tough, the tough get going...

Right?

You've heard this often enough that you likely do not question the validity of the *push harder* approach.

Well, pushing harder is probably a good approach if you're in the midst of mixed marital arts fight. It makes sense if you're trying to finish the last few miles of a marathon. It seems like a wise strategy if you're on the front lines of a battlefield.

But you're not, are you?

Your life is not a fight. Or a competition. Or a battle.

No one or no thing is pushing against you. Not the government. Not the credit card companies. Not your bank account. Not your spouse. Not your colleagues. Not your friends. Not your family. Not your children. Not your clients. Not your dreams. And certainly, the Universe never pushes against you in any way. There is no opponent, physical or non-physical, keeping you apart from your desires. The only thing between you and your desires — any desire that you could possibly imagine — *is your alignment with having it.*

Let that sink in for a moment.

A slight variation on the same point would be to say that the only thing keeping you from your desires is your resistance to having them. That's it. So when you drop the resistance, when you allow yourself to let go and relax enough to be a vibrational match for your desire, it's yours.

However, we're taught from an early age that in order to get what you really want, you must push through resistance, you must struggle and fight to reach the top, and you must sacrifice yourself in order to become deserving of your desires.

The logical approach (and ultimately the big fat lie) is that when you overcome the resistance in front of you, you are rewarded with your desires. But when you understand the metaphysics of our universe, there is only inclusion and no exclusion. In other words, there is no such thing as banishing something you don't like.

So when your approach to anything it to try to push through and overcome resistance, you will only see and experience more resistance because that's where you're choosing to focus. While these are just words to describe the mechanics of things, when you look at your own experiences, you know this to be true without exception.

When your default strategy to TRY HARDER kicks into gear, I am suggesting that you walk away from whatever you are doing and take a nap.

In a literal sense, taking a nap (or your nightly sleep) resets your vibrational momentum. It's the ultimate letting go. When you sleep, you drop all your resistance. As you consciously allow yourself to sleep and relax, you become an allower of your desires. So if you find yourself pushing, fighting, and trying to force an outcome, a nap is an excellent strategy. And if you're one of those people who resists napping because you believe you need to be productive all the time? Well, then you'd really benefit from allowing yourself to take a nap. But you'll have to experience the power of re-aligning yourself in this way rather than take my word for it.

I've used this strategy many times regarding one of my personal hot spots, technology. I run several websites and I know just enough about them to be dangerous. So when something goes wrong, my first inclination is always that the problem needs to be fixed, now.

So when things would break, I'd immediately dive into lines of code, start searching Google for answers, and fire off e-mails to tech support. I'd frenzy time and time again, even though my results were completely predictable from my past experiences. I fight a few hours, get nowhere, and finally give up out of frustration.

Having traveled down this dead end enough times, now when something goes wrong, the first thing I remind myself to do is back away. I get up from my desk and do something completely different, like taking a nap. Having practiced this, I am amazed at how many times the issue is completely resolved without me doing a thing. Things get back on track as a combination of my desire and me getting out of the way. It's wonderful (and completely counter-intuitive).

In a figurative sense, taking a nap means allowing yourself to take a break. Take a walk. Watch a good movie. Go have some fun. One of my most powerful allowing strategies is to take a vacation. There have been many times over the years when I've felt short on money and out of fear, my default strategy to *work harder* kicked in. Now, the results of this approach were the same as when I tried to fix my websites. There's a lot of dust and bluster, but nothing significant happens. I've learned that one of the most powerful things I can do to create money is to take a vacation. Really.

Time and time again, when I allow myself to get out of the physical and mental space of trying to fix whatever problem I'm focused on, including money, I become an allower of my desires. Over the years, lots and lots of money has appeared in my inbox while I was sitting on a beach, camping in the woods, or sitting on a chairlift. By relaxing and becoming a vibrational match for my desire (having money feels like relaxation and fun to me), the details get sorted out.

If this resonates with you, then before you allow yourself to take that nap, you may need to remind yourself of the fact that everything you want in your life feels like it's downstream from you. If you're reaching for something and it feels like you're fighting against the current to obtain something you want, then you know you've got resistance in your mix. In my own experience, even though I fully believe that everything I want is downstream, the conditioning to wrestle my problems to the ground in hopes of making them go away is deeply embedded.

Letting go requires a conscious decision. Giving up requires a leap of faith. So what I am saying here is that to experience this power, you'll need to hit the couch and see what happens. You might have to just shut down your computer and take the day (or week) off to do some totally fun stuff.

For you to experience the awesome feeling of relaxing into your desires, for it to hold any real meaning for you, you're going to have to allow yourself to experience the power of letting go. You can start by taking a nap.

CONTROL, NO. DIRECT, YES

IT's likely that you're focused on the thoughts of HOW desires will come into your life rather than living in the vibrational atmosphere of having your wants present in your life, now. Instead of living as if that thing you want is already here, and feeling that (the really efficient, metaphysically sound approach), our tendency is to focus on the absence of our desires and then spend time trying to strategize our way to manifesting them.

This is certainly understandable when you consider you've been trained to see yourself as the *doer* in your life. You likely see yourself as the one controlling your experiences, the one responsible for getting enough things done. So, if you want something to show up in your life, well, then you better start figuring out the proper strategy to get it, right? After all, that's clearly how things work, right?

Well, no.

When you stop and think about it, you already have 99% of the things you want in life. Really, you do. You just don't think about them because you just expect that those desires will manifest, and so they do. (By the way, it's worth taking a moment here to look around you and take note of all the wonderful things you've manifested in your life, everything from a cup of coffee to the bed you'll be sleeping in, to your first kiss — you've created all of it). The other 1% feels like more of a big deal only because you get in the habit of noticing (and consequently amplifying) its absence over time.

Let's make a critical distinction regarding your responsibilities as the deliberate creator of your reality. There's a powerful distinction between *controlling* your reality and *directing* your reality. Your job is to be the Director.

Let go of planning, figuring out, or attempting to control HOW your desire will come to you. Instead, start directing your reality by saying, what I want is done. I am not going to wait until this thing shows up to feel good. I am going feel good now, I am going to feel the presence of my desire now. I'm done waiting. Waiting to feel good keeps my desires just outside my grasp. I am ready to have what I want, now.

The Universe that's responding to each and every one of your desires does not see some of your desires as big and some as small. The Universe is only perfectly and mechanically reflecting back your vibration, so there's no difference between the creation of a glass of water or a billion dollars in your bank account. The only thing that determines whether either will show up in your experience is **the degree to which you expect and allow a particular desire**. For most people it's easy to expect and allow a glass of water but harder to expect and allow a billion dollars.

Remember, you have no idea how the apple you ate at lunch

expanded from a seed into something you like to eat. You do not really know how you came into this world. You likely have no idea how your car works. Or your cell phone. Or your TV. Or how a plane flies. You don't really know how the item you clicked on your phone screen one day makes its way to your home on the next. You don't really know why the sun appears. You just like that these things work for you; you're not spending any time worrying about HOW they work and so they meet your expectations and work. Over and over again.

Without realizing it, when you get up to fetch that glass of water, you are directing your reality. You're not fretting about pipes, reservoirs, pumps, or underground wells. When you get on a plane in New York and then get off in Chicago, you are directing your reality. You don't spend a minute trying to figure out and control how you got across the United States, you just expected it to happen. And when you direct your reality through your expectation, it always responds.

If I ask you to imagine having a billion dollars, there's an excellent chance that your first thought will be around how fantastical or unlikely this is to happen. Look deeper and you'll notice that in the moment, because you've not practiced imagining what this would feel like, your logical mind jumps in to take the steering wheel. Instead of imagining what having a billion dollars would feel like in meaningful, practical ways in your life, your focus turns to thought of HOW you would ever come into this kind of money.

Play along for a minute here. Ask yourself, How would I create a billion dollars?

While some ideas might flit through your mind, in the end I know what your answer will be.

I DON'T KNOW!

And that's exactly right. You *don't know* how to create a billion dollars. And you don't know how your refrigerator works. But you're not spending any time trying to figure out the latter; you just have a powerful desire for cold drinks. How your refrigerator works is none of your concern. The same is true for that billion dollars. It's none of your concern as to how it works. Really.

Here's why...

Start by allowing yourself to notice what it feels like when you're trying to control HOW something unfolds. You will notice there's a tightening within you. This feeling is an indicator of your resistance; a feeling that's rooted in your fear of your desire NOT happening. When you're trying to wrestle with how your desire comes into your life, you're really trying to wrestle NOT having something into submission. On a superficial level, these actions look right and seem logical, but we're interested only in how these actions feel at a vibrational level.

When you pay attention to how planning and strategizing feels, the vast majority of these actions are taken out of defensive postures undertaken to protect you from some unwanted outcome. Again, this makes perfect sense — we've been taught that it's our job to control our realities and avoid mistakes. But look deeper and you'll notice how often plans don't work out.

When I wrote *The Very Cool Life Code*, I was intent on making the book a success. While that was my intention, I couldn't just allow myself to say *this book is going to be a bestseller and that's that!* and bask in feeling. Instead of commanding my reality like a king, I chose to try to control it. I was afraid. I didn't want to feel the embarrassment of being a failed author, so I figured I would plan my way to success. I spent thousands of dollars with all sorts of marketers and put together a powerful offer to partner with about 25 other leaders in my industry, many of them friends. I sent them all copies of the book and my win-win offer if they would promote me. Such a wonderful plan.

No one accepted my offer. I'm sure it vibrated with my fear of failing. And so no one wanted to be a part of that. I hit my threshold of worrying and allowed myself to give up. I wanted the book to be successful, but I obviously had no idea how to make it so and I was tired of pushing so hard. I stopped resisting my thoughts of it being a flop and just allowed the idea that my book was going to be whatever it was going to be.

When I looked at my sales a few months later, I sold more books in a single day than I had in the previous three months. My book shot up to #1 on Amazon's bestseller list in the Happiness genre. I had no idea what was going on. I had moved on to other projects and stopped promoting my book in any way. A few days later, while thumbing through Oprah's magazine, I discovered a full-page ad for Dr. Phil's new book, *The Life Code*. When people looked up his book, they discovered my book. I surfed Dr. Phil's wave to the bestseller list.

Your job is never to control, to figure out, or to negotiate with your desires in any way. If you're afraid that somehow you cannot have your desire, you approach it from the vibration of desperation, and your desire will always move away. Conversely, notice that when you totally expect to get what you want (like a glass of water), you never try to unravel how it all occurs.

When you surrender to something in your life, you're not letting go of your desires. Rather, you're letting go of the need to control HOW your desire comes into your life. When you connect to a desire and you notice yourself asking HOW, this is your opportunity to tell the Universe what you will have. Be the king (or the queen)!

If you are now wondering HOW to do all of this right, HOW to let go and allow, right now would be a wonderful time to take a deep breath. As you exhale, declare to yourself that what you want is done. Then go play.

LET THE UNIVERSE SORT OUT THE DETAILS

TALKING to a friend's high-schooler son at a party, I heard the words tumble out of my mouth, and immediately regretted them.

"What do you plan on doing after you graduate?"

It's a common and innocuous question. I asked for the same reason people ask me, "So, what do you do, Drew?" It's a filler of conversational space.

For Kyle, the *right* answer would have been that he had been accepted to the university of his choice for pre-med or whatever. This would mean that he had a plan. In our culture, a good plan is the essential key to success. But Kyle looked me in the eye, started to laugh and said, *I don't really know what I want to do yet.* He was okay with the uncertainty of not having his entire life sketched out. I told him how refreshing I found his answer. Then I told him of my work with lawyers earlier in my coaching career.

Quite often, the lawyers' stories paralleled one another. In general, things had gone according to plan in their careers.

They'd been lawyers for a decade or two, they worked longer hours than they wanted, but in return they made enough money to justify those hours. Oh, and they also really didn't like being lawyers very much.

When I'd ask these people why they became lawyers, the common answer was a version of, *well, at the time, I didn't really know what else to do, and law school sounded like a good plan.*

There's nothing wrong with becoming a lawyer or having a plan. The point here is whether you are making decisions that feel aligned to you, or if you're making decisions just to have an answer, one that's socially acceptable. We've been trained that it's risky to live outside the certainty commonly associated with plans.

But look a little deeper and you'll see that most plans are put into place to protect you from the potential chaos of an uncertain future. In the example here, it's better to go to law school now than to risk taking being without a plan.

After all, you're supposed to control your future, right? You're supposed to have all the Whats, the Hows, and the Whens all figured out. You're supposed to go out and make it happen.

But the people who want you to get out there and make it happen have temporarily forgotten how cool it feels to *allow* it to happen. Look around and you just might notice that the people who try to control the Hows, the Whens, and the Wheres of their life are stressed out. When life strays from the plan as to how things were supposed to unfold (as life always does), there's another problem to solve.

The coolest things in my life — my relationship with my wife, my kids, my career, our wonderful home — came into my experience without me doing much. I knew the basic outlines of what I wanted, held steady to my vision of these things, and then they manifested in ways that were beyond anything I could have ever planned for.

It's totally possible (and I recommend) to just decide what you want and then let the Universe sort the details. Let. Go. You've already had many, many experiences like this in your life. You know how cool it feels to allow your desires. In my work, few things delight me more than hearing a client's *out of the blue* stories. They share how the money, the invitation, the lover, the object, or the opportunity they'd been wanting just showed up in the most unexpected, delightful way.

It's easy to attribute magical stories to luck, but when you understand the metaphysics of creation and dropping your resistance, you see that you're always creating your own luck. When you really allow yourself to surrender the control and management of your desires, things manifesting out of the blue is the rule, not the exception.

Now if getting your hands dirty in the details of managing your life feels like fun, I salute you. Plan away! My point here is to pay attention when you feel a desire welling up. If you notice that in the next moment you feel your energy drop because you don't know the *how* or the *when* or the *where* or the *why*, remember you can just let those questions go.

You don't have to rationalize your desires in order to have them. You don't have to figure out how to bring them into your life. You don't have to force the timing of anything. You can just allow them in the same way you've allowed so many good things into your life already.

We live in a vibrational universe — when it comes to the creation of things, everything starts off as a thought before it shows up in physical form. Your job is to tend to your vibration first.

You put yourself in a much stronger position if you spend time *imagining* yourself already having your desire — *what does it look like? feel like? smell like?* — rather than trying to figure out how to make it happen. This is especially true when you consider that when you stop and think about it, you most likely don't know HOW to make your desire happen. Otherwise you'd already have it, right?

Be willing not to know. Be willing to give up trying to control the details. Instead, decide that you can have whatever you want, just because you want it, and allow yourself to imagine what it feels like to have that desire, now. This is how you become a vibrational match to what you're asking for.

NO NEED TO PROVE YOURSELF

I LISTENED to an interview with the director Quentin Tarantino recently. He reflected back to a time when he was an aspiring filmmaker, talking to a friend about a particularly edgy opening scene he planned on writing for a movie one day.

Upon hearing his dream, one of his friends chimed in, "Man, they'll never let you do that!"

To this, a young Mr. Tarantino shot back, "Who's *they?*"

In the retelling this exchange, he was adamant.

"I've given no one that authority of *me*. *I* can do anything I want. *I* can achieve whatever *I* want to achieve. It's up to *me*. There is no *they*.

In fact, by saying there is a *they*, you create a *they*," he said.

He delivered these words with the power of a man who knew he was right. Because he was exactly right.

I am not suggesting that you raise both middle fingers in defiance of a world against you. You can do this, of course, but from a Universal perspective, when you start pushing against something, you get pushed back. Rather, instead of making *them* something to rail against, you just let *them* go. You can just let *them* be who they are. You can just make *them* irrelevant. As Tarantino astutely observed, you'll want to remember that *they* don't even exist.

That said, it's important to notice that your relationship to *them* can be quite subtle and rather complex. For example, for several decades, without realizing it, I was caught in the endless loop of trying to prove my success to *them*. After all, I'd made all these "radical" life decisions over the years. I left an academic career to start a coaching business. I started studying and sharing this woo-woo Law of Attraction stuff. When you live this far outside of the norm, certainly a segment of the population of *them* isn't going to like it very much. Right?

Well, this is what I believed.

Now the weird thing is that if you ask me who *they* were, I could not tell you. There was no specific person or group in my face who really cared about my decisions, there was no one really pushing against my ideas, there was nobody evaluating my level of success. No one but me.

Deep down, as a projection of my own lingering doubt about how good and easy my life could be, I felt the need to prove to *them* that my way was a viable, smarter, better way to live. In other words, the *they* I wanted to prove everything to?

That was really just me.

And when it comes to the notion of proving yourself? On a vibrational level, trying to prove something only demonstrates its absence. When you're in proving mode, you're really trying to protect yourself from NOT having something you don't want. You may want to read that last sentence again to take it in.

I continually tried to prove my success because deep down I was afraid of failing in the eyes of *them*. I never wanted to be seen as the lazy, irresponsible, pollyanna fuck-up that I assumed *they* believed me to be. However, when you're focused on protecting yourself from something unwanted, you invite more of that thing into your life. Even though I had everything I really desired in my life, something still always felt frustratingly outside of my grasp. I realized I was still making some of my decisions in an attempt to placate *them*. But because *they* don't really exist, they were impossible to placate. When you're running to prove yourself the treadmill never stops.

Looking at a common example, if you want a shiny luxury car in your driveway to prove your success to your neighbors and friends, vibrationally you are asserting that you currently don't have success. When that's your assertion, albeit unintentional, that car is going to be difficult to manifest. However if you want that shiny new car just because you really appreciate how wonderful that wooden steering wheel feels in your hand, you align yourself with the having of it. The point is that instead of trying to prove yourself, simply assert the presence of your desires now. Bask in that.

Back to the subject of *them*. It's wonderfully liberating to remember that there is no them. There is no one against you. Certainly the Universe operates tirelessly in the exact opposite manner, always helping you. There is no one or no thing outside of you that holds any authority over how you will choose to feel and what you decide you will have in your life.

Sure, some people (perhaps even family members and friends) will not agree with you or approve of your decisions or lifestyle. And yes, there are things like government institutions and corporations that churn out a never-ending series of rules and contracts to which they want you to adhere. But so what? You can always deal with those situations as they come up, simply by following what feels better to you in the moment. Fighting against them or trying to prove something to *them* is ultimately fighting yourself. Let *them* go.

They do not exist until the moment you choose to believe they exist. *They* are really just another one of you own creations. In fact, *they* are here to help you. *They* are projections of your own hidden fears that are more easily seen when attributed to other people outside yourself. And so when you feel like *they* are out to get you? Remember that this contrast is really serving as your opportunity to make a new decision as to what you will have going forward.

This is your unique life to create whatever it is that you desire. It will not look like anyone else's because you came here to discover and express your unique preferences. So get up, get out, and go live your life the way that YOU want to.

DECIDE

My three-year-old knows what he wants.

Most mornings when he wakes he tells me to fetch him two fig newtons. In fact, he orders me. He's usually not very polite. Sometimes I ask him to change his style of request and he repeats the nice words his mom and I taught him.

Regardless of how he asks, the underlying vibration of his request is the same — *I want two fig newtons and I will have them right now.*

His desire is clear. He's decided what he will have. He doesn't waver. He doesn't hope. He doesn't negotiate with his desire. He doesn't compromise his desire. He won't settle for one newton. His response is swift and clear — "TWO!"

And because his asking is so clear, his desire manifests. Of course the same is true for our baby girl. When she starts crying, indicating her clear desire to eat, to be changed, or to be held, everyone around her rushes to meet her request as quickly as possible.

All children are supreme manifestors. We all entered this world with the same clarity. We all came here to create the exact reality we want to experience. As we get older, our well-intentioned parents and teachers tell us the exact opposite. We learn we can't have everything we really want. We learn it's better to protect ourselves from our desires and not to expect too much (that way you won't go through the pain of disappointment). We learn that it's impolite to ask for what we really want. We learn to question our worthiness regarding our desires, and that we must somehow prove how we are deserving if we are ever to have what we want. We learn that we need to deal with reality as it is instead of being reminded that we are the sole creators of our reality.

As a result of all of this negotiating, you end up splitting your energy. And when you split your energy, you get uninspired results. For example, let's say you see that shiny new car and you feel the fire of desire. You want this beautiful car. Now in the moment of your pure desire, the car is yours. The deal is done. In some lot somewhere, the car is waiting for you to pick it up. If you stay in the unwavering clarity energy of your desire, it will show up in your experience just as easily as my son creates fig newtons.

But you don't usually get the car. What tends to happen much more often is that instead of deciding to have what we want, we immediately begin generating reasons why we cannot or should not have it.

I don't know how I would get the money to pay for it.

(My son has never concerned himself with any aspect of how the newtons make their way to the cupboard. And so, they are just always there to meet his clear expectation.)

I don't really need a new car. My old one is fine.

I don't want to think about what my friends and family would think about me if I had such a fancy car.

In each case, you see the energy of the original intention getting split from a simple *I want it* to the conflicted intentions of *I want it and I shouldn't want it.*

Remember the Universe is just an amplifying machine. It's not a judge. The Universe just reads your vibration and then amplifies. It's your personal concierge, unfailingly delivering your order. When you begin to compromise your desires and negotiate with yourself, you're choosing to order what you think you can get (e.g., "Maybe someday, I might be able to get a used version of the same car...") the likelihood of you manifesting what you want falls off the table.

So what's the remedy here?

Decide!

Decide what you really want.

Decide that you will have it.

The word decide comes from the Latin root *decidre* which means to cut off. So when you are making a decision, you are cutting off all unwanted possibilities. Let them go! You are going to have exactly what you want, just because you want it. No justifications. No explanations. No hoping.

When you decide what you want with the clarity and certainty of a king or a queen, you will see your desires begin to manifest. What you order and allow manifests. This is the Law of the Universe.

And no, it doesn't matter what desire you wish to create... It could be a leaner, healthier body, a fat bank account, or a hot lover in your bed. When you decide that you can and will have it, it's yours.

So working backwards, if you have a longstanding desire that just seems to remain frustratingly outside of your grasp, you know that you have not been truly deciding.

You did it at three. You can do it now.

YOUR PURPOSE IN LIFE: HAVE FUN!

Years ago I went to an amusement park with a roller-coaster loving friend. He insisted that we head right over to the park's biggest coaster, one of the most thrilling in the United States. When we reached the ride, there were two lines, one very long, and one quite short. Reflexively, I found a place in the short line, not noticing that my friend Warren had chosen the longer one.

"Drew, come over in this line. It's for the front car!" he said.

I yielded and met him in the longer line, but not quietly.

"Dude, why don't we just get in the other line?" I said. "We could ride this thing three times before we ever get on from the longer line."

Even though this event took place many years ago, I still hear Warren's reply in my head.

"Drew, do you want to ride 75% of the ride...? Or do you want to ride **100% of the ride**?" he said. "We came here for the fun of it, so let's have the most fun we can. Let's get in that front car, raise our hands in their air and let it rip around this place!"

And so we did. I smile just thinking back upon the memory.

You, me, everyone... We decided to incarnate into this physical form for the same reason we head to the amusement park — we came for the FUN of it. We came to get on this roller coaster and have the thrill of riding this sucker. Certainly, we all get to choose what percentage of the ride we wish to take — there is no getting it wrong — but since we're here, why not make it as thrilling as we can?

I tell this story to close this book as a simple reminder that the entire purpose of your life is to have fun. You decided to come here to experience the fun of seeing a constellation at night. You came to hear a small child's laughter. You came for the sunset over the ocean. You came to feel your lover's touch upon your thigh. You came to feel the cool breeze on a hot day. You came for the coffee. You came for the chocolate. You came for the sex. And you came for the roller coaster.

Conversely, it's important to mention the reasons you did not come here.

You did not come here to get life right.

(You could not possibly do it wrong).

You did not come to fulfill some duty to make the world a better place.

(The universe could not be any more perfect. The same is true for you.)

You did not come to search for some secret purpose.

(There is no such secret hiding from you, waiting to be uncovered).

You did not come to fulfill your potential.

(Your potential is limitless).

You did not come to learn lessons.

You did not come to prove yourself worthy.

You did not come here to try to suffer your way to happiness because deep down, you remember this to be a metaphysical impossibility.

You did not come here to spend your days trying to push a piece of string up a hill.

You did not come here to make things happen through your willpower or goal-setting or motivating yourself to do things you'd rather not do.

You are completely free to do all of these things of course, but when you really start paying attention to how it feels to be pushing yourself through life, it's not fun.

You came here for the exhilarating experience of creating your life through the power of focusing your thoughts. You came to give birth to new desires, and in doing so, you expand the entire realm of consciousness of the Universe. You came here for the roller coaster ride, reveling in the highs and then using the necessary lows as fuel to clarify your desires going forward.

If that seems too simple to you, you may want to ask yourself where you got such complicated ideas about life. Just because you've believed something for a long time does not make it true. In fact, you can always change your belief to match your new desire. It's never too late. So why not start with this these…

What if life was easy?

What if the whole point of your life was to allow yourself to have as much fun as you can?

Because do you know what happens when you allow yourself to have fun? You have fun.

You know what happens when you have fun? You re-wire yourself for fun. Fun finds you. Fun surrounds you. Everything you see is imprinted with the signature of fun.

Reading these words, as fantastic as they might seem, I bet you know them to be true. The theme is really allowing. Everything that you want in life is here for the taking. However, your desires manifest when you become a vibrational match to them. Your desires manifest when you start living your life at the *feeling* level of those desires.

You want certain things because you believe having them in your life would be more FUN. So now would be an excellent time to give up the strategy of trying to suffer your way to fun. Or to work your way to having fun later. Because here's the big secret (lean in close): Later never comes.

You read this book because you're interested in exploring ideas around making your life the best it can be.

So make it the best it can be NOW. Instead of pushing to get what you want, see what happens when you remember to let go of the fighting, the struggling, and the striving.

Let. It. Go.

ACKNOWLEDGMENTS

I've tried to express the ideas that inspired me through my own practice of easing into my deepest desires and share them with you in my own voice. A student and a teacher of The Law of Attraction for many years, I want to acknowledge the influence of two of my favorite teachers on the material in this book. First, the words and wisdom of Abraham-Hicks have served a source of great inspiration and laid the foundation for my understanding about the power of living deliberately.

Second, I would especially like to acknowledge my friendship with Frank Butterfield and his work with the Communion of Light over the past several years. My connection with Frank has led to some of the most profound insights of my life and many of the insights offered here can be traced back to conversations we've had over the years. The fingerprints of both sets of teachers can be found all over this book.

Further inspiration came during my 23rd or so viewing of one of my favorite films, Joel and Ethan Coen's masterpiece, *The Big Lebowski*. Over the years, the film achieved cult-like status, largely due to the main character's (Jeff Lebowski, aka "The

Dude") endearing "fuck it, let it go" ethos, shown in stark contrast to a world full of strivers and achievers. So, thanks to the Coen brothers and the actor Jeff Bridges for the message and the laughter.

Finally, this book has been filled with real world examples and personal stories to show you the power of letting go. In the case of client examples, to protect privacy, names and other characteristics are sometimes changed. In the case of my personal stories, everything is as I remember it. Thanks for reading my book.

— Drew Rozell, Ph.D.

North Hebron, NY

DID YOU LIKE THIS BOOK?

IF YOU ENJOYED THIS BOOK, please consider reading my other titles.

Visit www.verycoollifebooks.com for the complete bibliography and special offers.

REVIEW THE BOOK

If you liked this book enough to recommend it, please help me share my work with other like-minded people by leaving a review at the book's Amazon webpage, or in the e-book version, just scroll to the last page to be automatically directed.

Your reviews have a very powerful effect on book sales, so I thank you in advance.

YES, I WILL PERSONALLY COACH YOU

IF YOU RESONATED with this book, I'd love the opportunity to do what I do best — to personally coach you to integrate these ideas into your life.

To learn more about of my current personal coaching services and programs, please go to www.verycoollifebooks.com/coaching now and get in touch with me.

Please feel free to e-mail at drew@drewrozell.com.

I'd love to hear from you.

Printed in Poland
by Amazon Fulfillment
Poland Sp. z o.o., Wrocław
25 April 2023

8daa2be2-6656-471e-92df-8656ad543863R01

POSTMORTEM

CENTRAL CHANNEL BREATHING